CHARLES BOOTH'S POLICEMEN

Victor Bailey

♦

CHARLES BOOTH'S POLICEMEN

Crime, Police and Community in Jack-the-Ripper's London

BREVIARY STUFF PUBLICATIONS
2014

Published by Breviary Stuff Publications
BCM Breviary Stuff, London WC1N 3XX
www.breviarystuff.org.uk
Copyright © Victor Bailey, 2014
The centipede device copyright © Breviary Stuff Publications

A CIP record for this book is available from
The British Library

ISBN: 978-0-9570005-6-8

Images

Acknowledgements

The subject of this book was first explored some years ago in an inaugural lecture to mark my appointment as a distinguished professor at the University of Kansas. The research phase began when I held a visiting appointment at the Open University in England. I was inspired by the scholarship of Professor Rosemary O'Day and Dr. David Englander to look into the Charles Booth archive at the London School of Economics, upon which the present book draws. In the 1970s I was a graduate student with David at the Centre for the Study of Social History, University of Warwick. It was a pleasure to see him develop into an astoundingly good social historian before his untimely death in 1999, which was a considerable loss to the historical profession.

At the Open University, I was well placed to benefit from the historical wisdom of Professors Rosemary O'Day, Clive Emsley, and the late Arthur Marwick. I'm grateful to Professor Sir David Cannadine, then director of the Institute of Historical Research, for appointing me to a non-stipendiary research fellowship. A Fellowship from the National Endowment for the Humanities and a research grant from the National Science Foundation underwrote my extended visit to the Open University and the Institute of Historical Research. I doubt I would have secured either research award without the guidance of Kathy Porsch, grant development officer at the Hall Center for the Humanities.

The book was improved by the opportunity to present parts of the argument at the Law and Governance Conference at the University of Western Ontario in 2009, and at the Ninth European Social Science History Conference in Glasgow in 2012. Clive Emsley, Simon Stevenson, Joanne Klein, and Stefan Petrow kindly provided a critical reading of earlier drafts of the book. I alone am responsible for the outcome.

As Director of the Hall Center for the Humanities for the past thirteen years, I have had the great good fortune to be mentored by Charles Battey, chair of the Center's Advisory Board, whose name graces my professorship, and to be guided by Bill Hall, President of the Hall Family Foundation of Kansas

City. Jeanie Wulfkuhle, program administrator at the Hall Center, helped me with the illustrations, as did Sarah Williams, picture researcher at the Museum of London. Sally Utech, Hall Center associate director, held down the humanities fort while I struggled to finish the book. I am grateful to Mary Brooks for her indexing work and to Mary Johnson for her translation work. Paul Mangan of Breviary Stuff Publications was extremely indulgent when the essay I was composing burst the bounds of the collection for which it was intended. He instantly suggested it be published as its own volume, and was unfailingly responsive and helpful through the publishing process.

To my mother, Lily, I give thanks for a Yorkshire upbringing "with all its charm of direct thinking, honest work and warm feeling", if I may borrow Beatrice Webb's description of her northern cousins. In memory of my mother-in-law, Ruth, a Kansan of Welsh and English ancestry, I offer thanks for showing us how to remain active and full of curiosity in later life. To my wife, Ann-Kathryn, I dedicate this book for the love and sagacity she has generously bestowed on me for many a long year.

Charles Booth

CHARLES BOOTH'S POLICEMEN

Crime, Police and Community in Jack-the-Ripper's London

One of the most remarkable social characteristics of later Victorian England was the decline of recorded crime. The evidence of decline is compelling. Between the 1850s and the late 1890s, in the context of a doubling of the country's population, and a trebling of the specifically urban population, the rate of larcenies known to the police per 100,000 population fell by 52 per cent. Steep declines were likewise registered in reported robberies, in wounding offences, and in homicides. Adding the more serious of the non-indictable offences only confirms the steady decline in recorded crime. The rate of assaults (including common assaults, aggravated assaults, and assaults on the police) fell from 423 crimes per 100,000 people in 1875 to 204 crimes in 1900.[1] Even prosecutions for drunkenness and drunk and disorderly conduct (always more susceptible to variations in police, judicial and public activity) fell after 1875, and did not rise again until the end of the 1890s.[2] National

---

[1] V.A.C. Gatrell, "The Decline of Theft and Violence in Victorian and Edwardian England", in Gatrell et al (eds.), *Crime and The Law: The Social History of Crime in Western Europe since 1500* (London, 1980). The rates for burglary and house- and shop-breaking did not unambiguously fall, but they held steady. In the 1900s burglary and breaking offences rose: see "Decline", pp. 317-18; Clive Emsley, *Crime and Society in England 1750-1900* (Harlow, 2005), p. 32; William M. Meier, *Property Crime in London, 1850-present* (Basingstoke, 2011), p. 1.

[2] V.A.C. Gatrell and T.B. Hadden, "Criminal statistics and their interpretation", in E.A. Wrigley (ed.), *Nineteenth-century society* (Cambridge, 1972), p. 370; Gatrell, "Decline", p. 291.

statistics were strongly influenced by those for London, so the picture of declining crime rates was true also of the capital city.[3] The decline of crime and violence is extraordinary, and stands in stark contrast both to earlier and later periods of English history.

Are the recorded crime rates a valid measure of decline? Most historians think they are. Their argument goes as follows: when lawmakers were continuing to enlarge the boundaries of crime (criminalizing many forms of activity that had been unknown to the law), when the police were increasingly active in the enforcement of the law, when the public was increasingly cooperative with the law (willing to report and prosecute offenders), and when prisoners were released more rapidly or fined instead of imprisoned (providing them with more opportunity to commit crime), the recorded crime rates should have moved upwards. Since crime rates fell, it seems valid to conclude that the decline was a function more of actual behaviour than of changes in law, law enforcement, or public attitudes to crime.[4]

---

[3] D.J.V. Jones, *Crime, Protest, Community and Police in Nineteenth-Century Britain* (London, 1982), ch. 5; Stephen Inwood, *City of Cities. The Birth of Modern London* (Basingstoke, 2005), ch. 20. A decline in punishment paralleled this long decline in prosecution. Between 1871 and 1894, the population of convict prisons fell from almost 12,000 to less than 5,000. Between 1874 and 1893, the daily average prison population (in local and convict prisons) decreased from 29,000 to 13,300. This was due less to the decline in crime, however, since the committals to prison fell only slightly, and more to a decrease in the number of long sentences of penal servitude and imprisonment. See *Departmental Committee on Prisons*, Parliamentary Papers (PP) 1895, vol. LVI [C.7702] p. 407 and 539 (Troup).

[4] Gatrell, "Decline", passim. Not all historians agree that the "English miracle" was authentic. Jennifer Davis and Howard Taylor have both cast doubt on the veracity and reliability of the annual criminal returns. See J. Davis, "A Poor Man's System of Justice: The London Police Courts in the Second Half of the Nineteenth Century", *Historical Journal*, vol. 27 (1984), pp. 314-15; idem, "Prosecutions and Their Context: The Use of the Criminal Law in Later Nineteenth-Century London", in D. Hay and F. Snyder (eds.), *Policing and Prosecution in Britain 1750-1850* (Oxford, 1989), pp. 397-426; H. Taylor, "Rationing crime: the political economy of criminal statistics since the 1850s", *Economic History Review*, vol. LI (1998), pp. 569-90. For an effective rejoinder to Taylor, see R.M. Morris, "'Lies, damned lies and

The Victorians themselves were certainly convinced that there was much less crime than in earlier decades. As early as 1881, a London *Times* editorial declared: "Property, at the present day, is safer than it has ever been against depredations of every sort."[5] A year later, Howard Vincent, director of the criminal investigation department of the metropolitan police wrote: "London ... is the safest capital for life and property in the world."[6] In 1892, an assistant secretary of the Home Office wrote to the *Times*: "The very marked diminution in the number of persons known to the police as criminals ... are definite facts which corroborate the decrease in crime—prove in fact that it is a decaying branch of business."[7] And in 1901, the Criminal Registrar (in charge of the criminal records) claimed his era had "witnessed a great change in manners: the substitution of words without blows for blows without words; an approximation in the manners of different classes; a decline in the spirit of lawlessness."[8] The Victorians, one imagines, were not so blind to the social realities around them to have got the decline of lawlessness hopelessly wrong.[9]

What explains the pacification of later Victorian England? As yet, historians have done little more than offer macro-explanations for this greater law-abidingness: economic improvement, demographic change, changes in penal policy, or the imposition of alien values and an alien law on the poor through the work of social agencies and the police.[10] The most

criminal statistics': Reinterpreting the criminal statistics in England and Wales", *Crime, History & Societies*, vol. 5 (2001), p. 124.

[5] *Times*, 8 August 1881, p. 7. See also *Times*, 6 February 1899, p. 9.

[6] See "Vincent, Sir (Charles Edward) Howard", rev. C. Emsley, *Oxford Dictionary of National Biography* (Oxford, 2004, online edition).

[7] *Times*, 1 February 1892, p, 9, letter from "Inquirer."

[8] Cited in Gatrell, "Decline", p. 241.

[9] Of course Rob Sindall argued that Victorians based their beliefs about the state of crime, not on the actual state of crime, but on the official criminal statistics: *Street Violence in the Nineteenth Century: Media Panic or Real Danger?* (Leicester, 1990), p. 26.

[10] For the decline in the proportion of young men (the most criminogenic age group) in the population, from the very high levels of the 1820-1840 period, see E.A. Wrigley and R.S. Schofield, *The Population History of England*

provocative explanation is Professor Vic Gatrell's depiction of Victorian England as a "policeman-state." His case is that the police launched an intrusive, coercive, and predatory war on the poor and disadvantaged in the later Victorian years. If the initial impact of police surveillance was to dig deeper into the 'dark figure' of crime—to bring more criminals before the courts — the ultimate effect was an increase in general deterrence. Policing, we are told, established "a peculiar if transient advantage ... over ancient forms of popular lawlessness visible on the streets." The "policeman-state", he concluded, "really was enjoying an era of rare success."[11]

Gatrell's account received its most ringing endorsement in Stefan Petrow's study, *Policing Morals*, which examined how the metropolitan police were used to enforce a common morality. While Gatrell said little about the policing of the country's drunks, prostitutes, and gamblers, Petrow put them in his sight-line. The combination of "moral panics", moral vigilance bodies, and official responses to immorality so enlarged the powers of the metropolitan police, Petrow argued, that they became "a menacing and unwelcome presence in most working-class lives." "The cumulative impact of police powers", he declared, "was nightmarish." But is the "policeman-state" the soundest explanation of the law-abidingness of Victorian England?[12]

1541-1871 (Cambridge, 1981), pp. 7, 216. For the long decline in punishment, see D. Hay, "Time, Inequality, and Law's Violence", in A. Sarat and T.R. Kearns (eds.), *Law's Violence* (Ann Arbor, 1992), pp. 146-7.

[11] V.A.C. Gatrell, "Crime, authority and the policeman-state", in F.M.L. Thompson (ed.), *The Cambridge Social History of Britain 1750-1950* (Cambridge, 1990), vol. 3, pp. 243-310, at p. 292. In fairness, Gatrell has offered less polemical ways of explaining the decline of crime, as in "Decline", p. 258: "... there is little in a society's total experience which does not bear on the changing incidence of theft and violence within it: trends in crime are determined by the fine and shifting balance which prevails across a complex equation of crime-inducing and crime-inhibiting forces of great number."

[12] Stefan Petrow, *Policing Morals. The Metropolitan Police and the Home Office, 1870-1914* (Oxford, 1994), pp. 294-97. Again, in fairness, Petrow's conclusion accepts that there were "chinks" in the "disciplinary armoury of

For sure, the renowned social investigator, Charles Booth, ascribed the tranquility of London, and especially the East End of London in the 1890s, almost entirely to the physical presence of the police. Yet strangely, the evidence of Booth's police informants — to be examined closely in what follows — does not offer compelling support for Booth's conclusion. The present study advances the view that any convincing explanation of how social order was maintained in London requires a study of quite other forces and social arrangements. I have long been persuaded by Michael Ignatieff's proposition that "powers of moral and punitive enforcement are distributed throughout civil society", and by his call for a new social history which starts from "the assumption that a society is a densely woven fabric of permissions, prohibitions, obligations and rules, sustained and enforced at a thousand points rather than a neatly organized pyramid of power."[13]

An essential ingredient of this approach is an exploration of the division of labour between formal modes of criminal justice and the many local enforcers of norms. The hypothesis of this study is that the police operated within what Pierre Bourdieu called a 'force field', a social space endowed with its own rules and forms of authority, imposing specific determinations of variable intensity on those within the space, and yet also allowing improvisation and even escape from social conditioning.[14] The main agents within this zone of struggle included the beat policemen with their own operational practices, the "moral entrepreneurs" with their "civilizing efforts", the police court magistrates who scrutinized the policing of street crime, and inhabitants with their own codes, customs and culture. Without a

---

control", and that the police were not always the most zealous agents in the campaign against immorality.

[13] M. Ignatieff, "State, Civil Society, and Total Institutions: A Critique of Recent Social Histories of Punishment", in S Cohen and A. Scull (eds.), *Social Control and the State* (Oxford, 1986), p. 100. See also Ignatieff, "Total Institutions and Working Classes: A Review Essay", *History Workshop*, issue 15 (1983), pp. 170-71, 173.

[14] P. Bourdieu, *The Field of Cultural Production* (New York, 1993).

full appreciation of this force field, historians run the risk of overestimating the extent to which the police were able or willing to intervene in the daily behaviour of inhabitants in order to suppress law breaking. The police were not necessarily the prime movers in the social and cultural processes that restrained deviant behaviour. Rather, they were dependent upon individuals and agencies to bring them much of their business, and acted effectively only where the values that shaped their actions were generally shared. The commission and repression of crime are dependent variables. They are linked not only to the structures of law enforcement, but also to levels of community solidarity, associational life, family integration, and parental authority. They cannot be understood outside the history of employment, immigration, religion, charity, housing, and education.

I

A force field can be explored only within the environment where crime and control were negotiated daily.[15] The chosen ground for the present exploration is the East End of London. East London, which was much larger than the area known as the East End, had no clear and obvious boundaries. The municipal, parish, police, and police court jurisdictions did not coincide. Charles Booth's definition of East London was represented by a quadrant projecting three miles east of the City boundary. The radii of this quadrant were Kingsland Road going northwards and the River Thames running eastwards. Within this quadrant, Booth described an inner ring, ending at the Regent's Canal, and an outer ring, ending at the River Lea and Bow Creek. The inner ring of 1.5 miles, which Booth considered the 'heart' of the East End, included most of Shoreditch, Bethnal Green, and all of Whitechapel, St. George's-in-the-East, Wapping, Shadwell, and Ratcliff, and the west part of Mile End Old Town. The outer ring

---

[15] Dick Hobbs, *Doing the Business. Entrepreneurship, the Working Class, and Detectives in the East End of London* (Oxford, 1989), p. 14, makes the important methodological point: "… the status of criminal action needs to be looked at … from within the enacted environment where crime and control are negotiated day in, day out."

included Limehouse and Poplar, Bow, Bromley, the eastern extensions of Bethnal Green and Mile End, and most of Hackney. The entire area consisted of approximately 900,000 inhabitants in 1890. The inner ring of the East End consisted of roughly 500,000 people.[16]

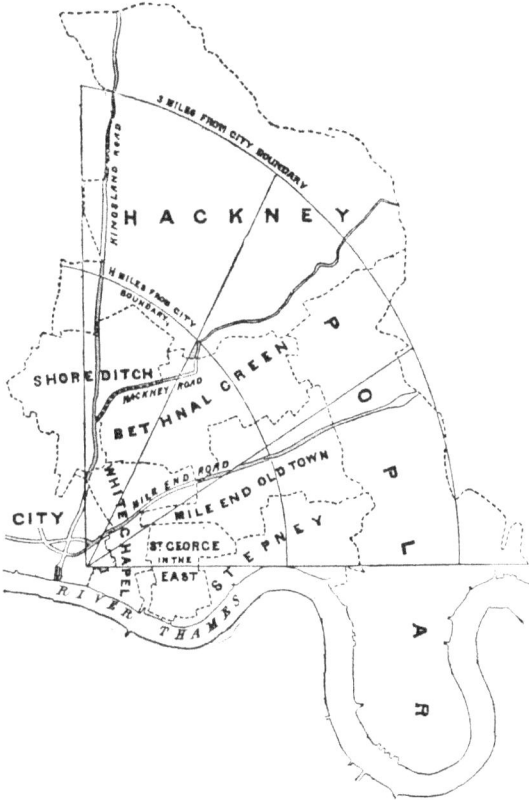

East London

In the inner ring, Bethnal Green's leading trades were

---

[16] Charles Booth, *Life and Labour of the People in London*, Poverty series, vol. 1 (London, 1902), pp. 29-30. See above for Booth's radial map. The first person to use the term "East-end" (sic) seems to have been social investigator, Henry Mayhew, in 1851. The *Oxford English Dictionary* gives 1883 as the date of first usage: see J. Green, *A Social History of the Jewish East End in London 1914-1939* (Lewiston, 1991), p. 4.

boot and shoe making and cabinet making. Women worked in matchbox, toy, and cardboard making. Not only was it overwhelmingly working class, but also ethnically homogeneous. Almost 99 per cent of those living in Bethnal Green in 1891 were British subjects, most of whom were native Londoners. Whitechapel and Spitalfields were noted for their Jewish (Russian-Polish) population, which dominated tailoring, boot making, and tobacco manufacturing. In St. George's-in-the-East, dock work, general waterside labour, and gas work employed most men, while women worked in sack making. Wapping and Shadwell were associated with dock work, riverside labour, and sailors. In the outer ring, in Poplar (including Bow & Bromley), men were employed mainly on dock, canal, railway, and gas work. A large percentage of married women in the East End were outworkers for various manufacturing trades — clothing, footwear, and matchbox making. Unmarried women were in factory jobs, such as jam, matches, or confectionery. There were also plenty of costermongers or street traders and small shopkeepers.[17]

By the later Victorian period, the East End had become notorious as a place of unalleviated poverty, crime and immorality, and the district where the issue of large-scale immigration was first confronted. From the 1870s, the East End was constructed as a heart of darkness, a place of *dis*ease, *dis*order, and *dis*tress, a breeding ground of the alien, whether Irish or Jewish, anarchist or socialist, criminal or pauper. Tales of

---

[17] See C. Booth, "Condition and Occupations of the People of East London and Hackney, 1887", *Journal of the Royal Statistical Society*, vol. LI (1888), pp. 276-80; Booth, *Life and Labour*, Poverty, vol. 1, pp. 63-72; *Report of the Royal Commission on Alien Immigration*, PP. 1903 [Cd. 1742], vol. IX, p. 361; C.T. Husbands, "East End Racism 1900-1980", *London Journal*, vol. 8 (1982), p. 6. The percentage of middle-class residents was small: 4.2% in Bethnal Green, 6.2% in Whitechapel, 2.5% in St. George's-in-the-East. See L. Marks, "Medical care for pauper mothers and their infants: poor law provision and local demand in east London, 1870-1929", *Economic History Review*, vol. XLVI (1993), p. 521; D.R. Green, "The Metropolitan Economy: Continuity and Change 1800-1939", in K. Hoggart and D. Green (eds.), *London. A New Metropolitan Geography* (London, 1991), p. 23.

expeditions into this part of the city were represented as crusades against the *terra incognita* of the urban slum. In the 1880s, though this imagery persisted, journalists, writers, and social reformers at least drew attention to the poverty, housing and underemployment of 'Outcast London.' So, too, Walter Besant's *All Sorts and Conditions of Men* underlined less the pauperism and crime and more the 'meanness' and 'monotony' of East End life. This less sensational picture of East End life was distorted afresh by the activities of Jack the Ripper in the summer and autumn of 1888. The five brutal murders of prostitutes reinforced the clichés of the East End as a social abyss, an urban jungle.[18]

The image of the East End as a nursery of pauperism and crime, a threat to the civilization of London and the Empire, provoked Charles Booth to choose the area for his first exploration into the conditions of the labouring poor. In an 1887 article read before the Royal Statistical Society, Booth justified his choice of the Tower Hamlets School Board Division for the first stage of his inquiry into the condition and occupations of the people of London by saying "that this piece of London is supposed to contain the most destitute population in England, and to be ... the focus of the problem of poverty in the midst of wealth, which is troubling the minds and hearts of so many people."[19] His remarks in the first volume of the Poverty series

---

[18] There is a vast literature on the East End as the heart of "Darkest London." For some of this literature, see P.J. Keating, *The working classes in Victorian fiction* (London, 1971), pp. 105-7; D.E. Nord, "The Social Explorer as Anthropologist: Victorian Travellers among the Urban Poor", in W. Sharpe and L. Wallock (eds.), *Visions of the Modern City* (Baltimore, 1987), pp. 123-4; J. McLaughlin, *Writing the Urban Jungle* (Charlottesville, 2000), p.126. See also Arthur Morrison, *A Child of the Jago* (London, 1996; first pub. 1896); idem., *Tales of Mean Streets* (London, 1894); Jack London, *The People of the Abyss* (New York, 1907; first pub. 1903). East London got so tired of the regular influx of social observers and press voyeurs that an East London Defence Alliance was formed in 1886 to protect the region from philanthropists and journalists: see J. Davis, *Reforming London. The London Government Problem, 1855-1900* (Oxford, 1988).

[19] C. Booth, "The Inhabitants of Tower Hamlets (School Board Division), their Condition and Occupations", *Journal of the Royal Statistical Society*, vol. 50 (1887), p. 374. See also Beatrice Webb, *My Apprenticeship*

further revealed the intent of the inquiry:

> East London lay hidden from view behind a curtain on which were painted terrible pictures: — Starving children, suffering women, overworked men; horrors of drunkenness and vice; monsters and demons of inhumanity; giants of disease and despair. Did these pictures truly represent what lay behind, or did they bear to the facts a relation similar to that which the pictures outside a booth at some country fair bear to the performance or show within? This curtain we have tried to lift.[20]

The East End became a laboratory, then, for social investigators, social workers, and philanthropists, whose rich archives are now available to the historian.[21] No archive has been of greater value than that of Charles Booth, principal investigator for, and lead author of, the seventeen-volume *Life and Labour of the People in London* (1889-1903), which one of his assistants, Beatrice Webb, described as "the grand inquest into the conditions of life and labour of the four million inhabitants of the richest city in the world."[22] Booth's survey was divided into three separate but overlapping series: *Poverty*, *Industry*, and *Religious Influences*. The third series examined "the action of organized

---

(Harmondsworth, 1971; first pub. 1926), p. 233.

[20] Booth, *Life and Labour*, Poverty, vol. 1, p.172.

[21] Husbands, "East End Racism", p. 3.

[22] Webb, *Apprenticeship*, p. 226. In the last of the 17 volumes, Booth stated: "the object of the sixteen volumes has been to describe London as it appeared in the last decade of the nineteenth century": see Mary Macauley Booth, *Charles Booth. A Memoir* (London, 1918), p. 135. Beatrice Webb described Charles Booth as "perhaps the most perfect embodiment of what I have described ... as the mid-Victorian time-spirit — the union of faith in the scientific method with the transference of the emotion of self-sacrificing service from God to man": *Apprenticeship*, p. 230. *Life and Labour* has been described as "the first great empirical study in the social survey tradition": M. Bulmer, K. Bales, K.K. Sklar, "The social survey in historical perspective", in Bulmer et al (eds.), *The social survey in historical perspective 1880-1940* (Cambridge, 1991), p. 19. The best account of *Life and Labour* is R. O'Day and D. Englander, *Mr. Charles Booth's Inquiry* (London, 1993).

religion in all its forms", that of "other organized social and philanthropic influences" and the public authorities (including the police), and social conditions that the previous series had neglected, such as drink, prostitution and crime.[23]

At the back of the third series on Religious Influences is a large archive of unpublished materials. Of particular importance for this study are the "police walks", which came into being between 1897 and 1902. Booth's team of investigators first set up camp north of the Thames in 1897-8, starting in the Isle of Dogs and working west to Hackney. They then moved to the inner ring of London north of the Thames. "Our plan of action", said Booth, "may be likened to a voyage of discovery. We have moved our camp from centre to centre all over London, remaining for weeks or even months in each spot in order to see as well as hear all we could." "In our prolonged walks through London", Booth added, "walks to be measured by hundreds, or even thousands, of miles — we had ... the company and co-operation of experienced members of the Police force, chosen for their local knowledge." In the course of these walks, the police were "our 'guides, philosophers and friends'," and "almost every social influence was discussed, and especially those bearing upon vice and crime, drunkenness and disorder."[24]

---

[23] Booth devoted almost half the 17 volumes of *Life and Labour* to "Religious Influences." Booth himself was raised a Unitarian.

[24] Booth, *Life and Labour*, Religious Influences, vol. 1, p. 7; *Life and Labour*, Final volume, p. 136. See also O'Day and Englander, *Inquiry*, pp. 6-7; R. O'Day and D. Englander, "Interviews and investigations: Charles Booth and the making of the Religious Influences survey", in Englander & O'Day (eds.), *Retrieved Riches: social investigation in Britain 1840-1914* (Aldershot, 1995), pp. 143-57. There was a long tradition of metropolitan policemen, uniform and detective, acting as guides to slumming parties (though Sir Edward Bradford did away with the practice at the turn of the century), and as a source of social observation. Policemen gave evidence to all the principal parliamentary inquiries of the period on questions of immigration, housing, sweating, street trading and drunkenness. As the primary agents of order in daily touch with the public, the police were thought to possess an expertise that was empirical, concrete and communal. The police walks for the Booth survey are in keeping with this tradition. The policemen supplied local knowledge of the area and inhabitants, and, if necessary, provided protection. See Josiah Flynt, "Police Methods in London", *The North*

Descriptive map of London Poverty: East London sections, 1889

Booth's associate, George Duckworth, half-brother of Virginia Woolf, undertook the bulk of the police walks. Educated at Eton and Cambridge, Duckworth was from the upper levels of the professional middle class. He was said by Booth to have an eye for detail and sound judgment, the accuracy of which is borne out by Duckworth's highly readable reports.[25] It should be noted immediately that the detailed notes on the appearance of houses and streets, which the police helped to inform, were used to revise the Poverty Maps of 1889 (which had been based on the more labour-intensive method of house-to-house reports from School Board Officers). Duckworth's peregrinations made possible a systematic revision of the social classification of

American Review, vol. CLXXVI (1903), p. 437; Montagu Williams, *Round London. Down East and Up West* (London, 1892), p. 76.

[25] For Duckworth, see A. and V. Palmer, *Who's Who in Bloomsbury* (Brighton, 1987), pp. 44-5; *Times*, 28 April 1934, p. 14 (obituary); 30 April 1934, p. 16 (H.A.L Fisher letter); Leonard Woolf, *An Autobiography* (Oxford, 1980), vol. 2, p. 50; K. Bales, "Lives and Labours in the Emergence of Organised Social Research, 1886-1907", *Journal of Historical Sociology*, vol. 9 (1996), p. 125.

London streets. In addition to asking his police guides about the classification of streets, upon which revised poverty maps were based, Duckworth interrogated the police concerning the nature of prostitution in different districts, the incidence of gambling, the extent of drinking, and police relations with publicans. Little of this material, especially on morals offences, found its way into the published volumes of *Life and Labour*. As such, the unpublished notes of the police walks are a valuable and relatively unexploited resource for the study of London policing.[26] Indeed, I would argue that they provide one of the most important compilations of testimony that we possess for the policing of Victorian London.

Yet the police notes must be used with discrimination. There are no verbatim transcripts of the comments of either police or clerical informants; only Duckworth's paraphrase of the ambulant conversation, snippets of the policemen's words that Duckworth chose to quote, and his rare remarks on the idiosyncracies of his informants.[27] The police who escorted Duckworth round the East End were drawn largely from the higher ranks of each division. Of the dozen policemen involved, two-thirds were inspectors, one-quarter were superintendents, the latter being the highest post that a man starting as an ordinary constable could rise to. Little was heard from the lower ranks:

---

[26] The police walks for the East End of London are in Booth Collection, Notebooks relating to the Religious Influences Series, Police Walks, B 346-B 355, British Library of Political and Economic Science, London School of Economics. I have occasionally used evidence from policemen who were serving in other parts of London, though in most instances these men had spent some part of their police career in the East End.

[27] The police informants come to life through Duckworth's thumbnail sketches. Superintendent Mulvaney from Whitechapel was described as "a man rather over 50, blackish beard, medium height, inclined to drop his h's tho' not so much as Supt. Weston, spits frequently. Very friendly & anxious to do anything in his power to help. Had never before seen the map shewing the streets coloured according to character & was very much struck by it." P.C. Ryeland from Hoxton was 40-45 years of age, a temperance enthusiast. Inspector Pearn from Bethnal Green was "rather pompous but a good fellow." See Police Walks, B 350, folio. 43 (Mulvaney); B 352, folio 71 (Ryeland); B 349, folio 217 (Pearn).

only one escort was a police constable and one a sergeant, and very few police escorts were detectives. This ensured experienced informants, with many of them having twenty years service in the force. Moreover, since police service recruitment at divisional level was based on a single-tier entry system, officers would have had a close understanding of the experiences and practices of the man on the beat. While skeptical of some of what he heard, Duckworth never suggested that police remarks were related to rank. The information in the notebooks is reasonably representative, then, of police attitudes and opinion.[28]

It was evident that the Chief Commissioner of Police had encouraged the fullest cooperation with the Booth team. Superintendent Ferrett from Paddington informed Duckworth: "'Sir Edward [Bradford, Chief Commissioner of Police] told me that this survey of Mr. Booth's was a work of national, he even said international importance & that every possible assistance was to be given.'"[29] Occasionally resistance was met, though Duckworth always seemed wise to it. Inspector Fitzgerald took Duckworth round part of Hackney near Victoria Park. Duckworth noted that it all looked "rather vicious, though Fitzgerald would not admit it. He was very reticent on these questions & had apparently received some warning from his superiors on the subject." He also denied that constables were given either beer or money by publicans, but Duckworth added: "Fitzgerald was very uncomfortable during the questions which may have been natural nervousness but rather gave the impression that he was putting his estimate of police integrity too high."[30]

There is little question that Duckworth was influenced in

[28] See D. Englander, "Policing the Ghetto: Jewish East London, 1880-1920", *Crime, History & Societies*, vol. 14 (2010), pp. 35-6.
[29] Police Walks, B 359, f. 217. Bradford was Chief Commissioner from 1890 to 1903. See also Superintendent Weston (Bethnal Green), who said "that it was Sir Edward Bradford's special wish that the best men should be placed at Mr. Booth's disposal": Police Walks, B 347, f. 145.
[30] Police Walks, B 346, f. 51; B 347, f. 60. Duckworth described Fitzgerald, an Irishman, as "A bit of a blarney. Has been in the district 3 years but does not know it particularly well": B. 346, f. 157.

his summary description of each district by the police code of street life. Police informants categorized streets less in terms of 'poverty' and more of 'respectability' or 'roughness', for which they had a set of surrogate moral and material measures. Clean curtains, neat window boxes, the residence of policemen in the street all denoted respectability; broken windows, unshod and dirty children, 'apronless women', and street mess were sure signs of rough life. In the same vein, common lodging houses indicated the presence of thieves, prostitutes and roughs.[31] Of course, this was no mirror-image of London, but one shot through with the personal, occupational, and class attitudes of the police guides.

It is this code of the streets, moreover, which was adopted by Booth in the later published volumes of *Life and Labour*. As David Reeder persuasively argued, Booth identified from the police notes "a string of degraded streets across London sharing common characteristics."[32] All were colour-coded black and blue. All were "rough", given to public brawling and domestic violence; "low", with poor social habits, and "vicious", or semi-criminal and the locale of prostitutes. According to the police notes, for example, the streets in the Fenian Barracks had all the signs of vicious poverty: drunken women, truanting children, no tradition of respectable family life.[33] In short, Booth constructs a picture of a "residuum" combining his Class A (vicious and semi-criminal) and Class B (those who scraped a living from casual work and charity). In the East End as a whole, according to Booth, the residuum was 13.2 per cent of the population, though in Bethnal Green the figure rose to 17.2 per

[31] See D. Reeder, "Representations of metropolis: descriptions of the social environment in *Life and Labour*" in Englander & O'Day, *Retrieved Riches*, pp. 326-28. As an example of the police and Duckworth at work re-colouring the streets of the Poverty Map, see Police Walks, B 350, f. 184 (Inspector Drew, St. George's-in-the-East).

[32] Reeder, "Representations", pp. 331ff. See also Booth, *Life and Labour*, Religious Influences, vol. 2, p. 99: "Broken windows are one of the surest signs of rough life."

[33] Reeder, ibid. See also Ellen Ross, "'Not the Sort that Would Sit on the Doorstep;' Respectability in Pre-World War 1 London Neighborhoods", *International Labor & Working Class History*, vol. 27 (1985), pp. 42, 49.

cent. The relatively small concentrations in the lowest classes inspired Booth to argue that Class A had to be "harried out of existence" by the enforcement of sanitary, police and school regulations (including slum clearance), and that Class B had to be removed from the scene by the 'state socialist' solution of labour colonies, if there was to be any hope of restoring the fortunes of the respectable working classes.[34]

All this must be taken into consideration when using the material in the police walks. Yet if the purpose of the police walks was largely to inform the revision of the 1889 Poverty Maps, if the police guides accentuated Booth's preoccupation with a semi-criminal residuum, the evidence within the police notes also lays bare the working lives and practices of the metropolitan police, as well as the attitudes and assumptions of the police toward the habits and mentalities of their habitual customers. The notes, in short, get us as close to everyday police work and assumptions as we are likely to get. Before moving to this evidence, however, we first need to offer a guide to the organizational framework and principal mission of metropolitan policing.

---

[34] Booth, *Life and Labour*, Poverty, vol. 1, pp. 33ff and 174-5. Booth classified the London population (more strictly individual households) into eight classes, labeled A to H. He distinguished the poor (A-D) from the better-paid and regularly-employed working classes (E-F), and he separated the deserving poor (C-D) from the undeserving (class B) and the vicious, semi-criminal (class A). As Richard Dennis said, Booth "was reformulating old impressions (the idea of the 'savage' outcast residuum, the contrast between 'deserving' and 'undeserving') as new scientifically demonstrated certainties": *Cities in Modernity. Representations and Productions of Metropolitan Space, 1840-1930* (Cambridge, 2008), p. 70. Booth's street-by-street mapping used seven colours to indicate a street's position on the poverty scale. The very poorest areas were coloured black. See also G. Himmelfarb, *Poverty and Compassion* (New York, 1991), pp. 108ff; C. Topalov, "The city as *terra incognita*: Charles Booth's poverty survey and the people of London, 1886-1891", *Planning Perspectives*, vol. 8 (1993), 395-425; Jose Harris, "Between civic virtue and Social Darwinism: the concept of the residuum", in Englander & O'Day, *Retrieved Riches*, pp. 78-82; S. Joyce, *Capital Offences. Geographies of Class and Crime in Victorian London* (Charlottesville, 2003), p. 213.

II

London was heavily policed. Of the 35,000 policemen in the country in 1886, 14,700 were in the metropolis, which meant that 42 per cent of all policemen were policing a capital city that was home to 18 per cent of the population.[35] At ground level, in H division, or Whitechapel, an area of two square miles, there were in the 1890s between 570 and 590 policemen of all ranks for a population of approximately 76,000, or one policeman for 131 inhabitants, making it a heavily policed East End district.[36] Most recruits to the metropolitan police were aged 22 or 23, were at least 5' 9" in height, and were farm labourers and servants or rural craftsmen, attracted by the wages and working conditions. Rural recruits were thought to have the strong and healthy physique required for daily patrolling, and to have no ties to the people they would need to patrol. During the next two decades, the profile would change, as more recruits were drawn from those who were born, resided or worked in London (from 39 per cent in 1889 to 58 per cent in 1905).[37] The policeman's wage in 1890

---

[35] D.J.V. Jones, *Crime, Protest*, p. 137; Gatrell, "Decline", p. 275. Metropolitan police strength held steady in the late Victorian years. There was one policeman for 420 London inhabitants in 1871, one per 466 in 1881, and, following a notable increase in police numbers between 1882 and 1884 (in response to a spate of armed burglaries and concerns about Fenian activities) and in 1886-87 and 1889-90 (in response to unemployed demonstrations and the Dock Strike), one per 421 inhabitants in 1891. Of the nearly 15,000 men serving in the metropolitan police division in the 1890s, approximately 12,500 were constables, 1,700 were sergeants, 720 were inspectors, and 31 were superintendents. All the officers had risen from the rank of constable. The superintendent was responsible for the condition of an entire district (and there were 21 land districts or 'divisions'); the inspectors directed the sergeants in each section of a division; and the sergeants assigned constables to the beats of each section.

[36] PP. 1888 (416), vol. LXXXII, pp. 2-3; "Return of the Men of All Ranks in each Division;" Police Walks, B 151, f. 43.

[37] This led perhaps to Superintendent Smith's lament in the late 1890s that "he would rather have them uneducated & willing to do what they are told without thinking than the Board-School-educated man they get today." The proportion of recruits from the army was surprisingly low, the percentage of total strength ranging from 9.5 in 1875 to 15.4 in 1894. But as chief commissioner Monro wrote, "military duty is necessarily unbending – police

started at 24 shillings a week, a wage equivalent to that of an unskilled labourer. His pay rose by one shilling a week per annum to 30 shillings after five years, though this was before deductions for pension. Married constables (and three quarters of policemen were married) received a weekly lodging allowance and a clothes allowance, but wives were not allowed to work, a policy designed to mark the moral distance that was expected between police families and the neighbourhood poor.[38]

The requirement of working-class respectability also lay behind the insistence that married men live near the station in a neighbourhood free of criminal taint. As Booth was told: "a policeman may not live in a slum." He could live in overcrowded accommodation, however, since a quarter of the force did so. In the more crowded parts of London, said Booth, "the choice is almost limited to the better class of block dwellings."[39] Indeed, policemen were the fourth-largest occupational group amongst the tenants of the Peabody Buildings in 1891. Otherwise, policemen lived in respectable working-class streets, alongside Booth's classes E and F, or the artisans of London's workforce. Single policemen lodged in the homes of fellow policemen, or, more frequently, in section houses. In the Leman Street subdivision of Whitechapel, for example, one-third of the strength was in the section house. Booth judged the policeman's condition in 1894 "equal to that of most skilled workmen", but this was true only when rent and clothing allowances and pension

---

work is as necessarily elastic." "An army of military police" would be out of place in the crowded streets of London: Police Walks, B 355, f. 190 (Smith, C Division); B 151, f. 46; James Monro, "The London Police", *North American Review*, vol. 151 (1890), p. 621.

[38] I have relied heavily in this section on H. Shpayer-Makov's superb labour history of the metropolitan force, *The Making of a Policeman: a social history of a labour force in metropolitan London, 1829-1914* (Aldershot, 2002), passim; and idem., "The Appeal of Country Workers: the Case of the Metropolitan Police", *Historical Research*, vol. LXIV (1991). The rate of policemen's wives' employment was 2.3% in 1887: A. August, *Poor Women's Lives. Gender, Work, and Poverty in Late-Victorian London* (London, 1999), p. 169.

[39] Police Walks, B 151, f. 25 (Inspector Hodder); Booth, *Life and Labour, Industry*, vol. 8, p. 53.

were factored in.[40] Sergeants earned 35 shillings or more, a weekly wage that was equivalent to that of a skilled artisan.

The official training period was remarkably brief; no more than three to five weeks, most of which time was spent on drilling parades, little on instruction in police duties. The recruit was then sent to a division to learn from personal experience. The new constable was initially sent out on the streets accompanied by an experienced constable, who doubtless imparted the lore as well as the law of street policing. But soon he was alone. As Benjamin Leeson, posted to Whitechapel in 1891, wrote: "my third Sunday in the Force saw me working a beat, to all intents and purposes a fully qualified 'bobby.'"[41] The average day beat was seven and a half miles; the average night beat was two miles. Both were traversed at a rate of two and half miles an hour. In addition, there was an extensive system of fixed points or sentry duty, which restricted policemen to 100 yards in any direction, except when called away, providing ready public access to a policeman

---

[40] A. Newsholme, "The Vital Statistics of Peabody Buildings and other Artisans' and Labourers' Block Dwellings", *Journal of the Royal Statistical Society*, vol. 54 (1891), p. 90; C.H. Rolph, *London Particulars* (Oxford, 1980), p. 1; Jerry White, *Rothschild Buildings. Life in an East End tenement block 1887-1920* (London, 1980), p. 24. Agitation over pay and pensions suggests that not all policemen felt well off. In 1872, a mass meeting of constables and sergeants led to a pay rise (and to constables being discharged for insubordination); in 1890, a police strike led to another pay rise and to the grant of a pension for life for those who completed 25 years' service, a demand openly seconded by the Chief Commissioner of Police, James Monro, who resigned over what he deemed his failure to achieve improved pay and pensions: Shpayer-Makov, "The Appeal", p. 191; National Archives (NA), MEPO 2/147; MEPO 2/227; HO 45/9707/A50657; HO 45/9708/A50838; *Times*, 13 June 1890, p. 9; J. Timewell, *The Police and the Public* (London, 1898), p. 14; J.P. Martin and G. Wilson, *The Police: A Study in Manpower* (London, 1969), p. 17.

[41] Leeson, *Lost London. The Memoirs of an East End Detective* (London, 1934), p. 37. See also "The Police of London", *Quarterly Review*, vol. 129 (1870), p. 128; Frederick P. Wensley, *Forty Years of Scotland Yard* (New York, 1968; first pub. 1930), chap. 1; Monro, "London Police", p. 622; Tom Divall, *Scoundrels and Scallywags* (London, 1929), p. 12; Shpayer-Makov, *Making*, pp. 100-103; Shpayer-Makov, *The Ascent of the Detectives* (Oxford, 2011), p. 95; Gatrell, "policeman-state", p. 272.

in inner city areas. Fixed point duty was disliked, and was thought to make men more open to temptation from bribes, but they continued to be sited next to what were considered to be the roughest and rowdiest inhabitants. Inspector Weston told Duckworth that there were many fixed points in Bethnal Green, though he personally favoured short patrols. Finally, night patrols were put on in districts where people stayed up late or were especially noisy.[42]

One month's day duty was followed by two months of night duty. Three fifths of the force was on duty at night, when visits by sergeants and inspectors were more frequent. The largest number of police was in the streets between 10 p.m and 1 a.m., since the night men were on duty and the patrols and point men had not gone off. Extra force was available when, as Booth said, "the population on pleasure bent, order is most liable to be disturbed."[43] The eight consecutive night hours from 10 p.m. to 6 a.m. were said to make "a heavy call upon the endurance of the novice."[44] The other two-fifths of the force was on duty during the sixteen hours of the day in alternate watches of four hours each (so that only one-fifth of the London force, or say 3,000 policemen, was on duty at any time during the day).

Police work took its toll on health. In many years a half or more of the authorized strength was on the sick list at some

---

[42] C. Emsley, *The English Police* (London, 1991), p. 208; J. White, "Police and People in London in the 1930s", *Oral History*, vol. 11 (1983), p. 35; Police Walks, B 350, f. 37 (Weston); B 352, f. 105 (Ryeland).

[43] Booth, *Life and Labour*, Industry, vol. 8, p. 48. See also "The Policeman's Diary", *All the Year Round*, 5 January 1889, pp. 8-9; Police Walks, B 151, f. 26; B 347, f. 189 (Fitzgerald); Shpayer-Makov, *Making*, p. 133.

[44] Shpayer-Makov, ibid. There was parade before and after the beat, there were reports to write and court sessions to attend. If a man arrested a person on night duty, he would go off duty at 6 in the morning, but have to be at the police court at 10 o'clock. It was not unusual, therefore, for constables to work 60 or even 70 hours a week. A man was rarely transferred out of his division, but his beat or point was changed monthly, so that he worked in every part of the division in the course of two to three years. The aim was to prevent a constable from getting too "thick" with any particular people, and to make it harder for him to be bribed by publican or prostitute.

point in the year. Long hours in bad weather resulted in "diseases of exposure" (rheumatism, bronchitis, and tonsillitis), and policemen suffered what Leeson described as "a good hiding at more or less regular intervals."[45] Recorded assaults against policemen declined from the 1850s, but at century's end 2,700 London policemen were still being assaulted each year in execution of their duty, representing 20 per cent of the entire force. According to the superintendent of the Whitechapel division, 40 per cent of his men were assaulted in 1889, one half of who fetched up on the sick list.[46]

And discipline was stringent. "Few slips are allowed the P.C.", said Hugh Gamon, who took up residence in East London for his study of the police and police courts; "he walks in fear of degradation and dismissal, and dismissal carries with it loss of the pension." This level of work discipline compelled officers to internalize the values and code of practice of the police, and removed the policeman from a close connection with working-class culture. As Gamon said, the life of the policeman was a life apart: "Living with the people, but not of the people, they feel like a mercenary force quartered in a strange and alien land. They have distinct aims, sympathies, and ideas. They form a self-contained whole independent of the neighbourhood in which they move."[47]

---

[45] Leeson, *Lost London*, p. 37. For the toll on health, see H. Shpayer-Makov, "Police Service in Victorian and Edwardian London: A Some-what Atypical Case of a Hazardous Occupation", *Medizin Gesellschaft und Geschichte*, vol. 13 (1995), pp. 65-79.

[46] Gatrell, "policeman-state", pp. 276, 286; Shpayer-Makov, *Making*, p. 140; Emsley, *English Police*, p. 214; Monro, "London Police", p. 624; NA, MEPO 2/752; F.P Wensley, *Detective Days. The Record of Forty-two Years' Service in the Criminal Investigation Department* (London, 1931), p. 289; M. Clapson and C. Emsley, "Street, Beat, and Respectability: The Culture and Self-Image of the Late Victorian and Edwardian Urban Policeman", in *Policing and War in Europe*, ed. L. Knafla, *Criminal Justice History*, vol. 16 (2002), p. 122.

[47] R.P. Gamon, *The London Police Court To-Day & To-Morrow* (London, 1907), pp. 26-7. Between 1900 and 1910, up to 11 per cent of the metropolitan force was being disciplined each year. See also Gatrell, "policeman-state", p. 274; Shpayer-Makov, *Making*, pp. 78, 261. And cf. C.

In addition to the uniformed constabulary, there were a small number of detectives. In the 1870s, 2.4 per cent of the metropolitan force was employed in detective work; by 1914 this had risen only marginally to 3.6 per cent, or 729 men. Detectives were recruited from the uniformed rank-and-file by examination. Those recruited tended to have some experience of living or working in London before joining the police, and if the bulk of detectives were from the lower rungs of the social ladder, more came from non-manual occupations than was the case with uniformed constables. Entry into detective ranks was typically prefaced by a stint in plain-clothes work. Plain-clothes men were assigned, especially during the winter months, to clear the streets of special nuisances: begging, street betting, and prostitution. The bulk of detective work was done by divisional detectives, men permanently attached to each division, under the control of the divisional superintendent.[48]

The early morning parade over, the uniformed police took to the streets. E. Buxton Conway described the scene in a chapter of George Sims's *Living London* (1901):

> ... the long line of constables, marching in close single file, emerges, snake-like, from the gateway into the street. Taking the edge of the pavement, the file swings along under the charge of a sergeant or acting sergeant, who marches beside it. As each duty-post is reached, the rear man of the little procession 'falls out', until

Steedman, *The Radical Soldier's Tale. John Pearman, 1819-1908* (London, 1988), pp. 57-8. The very act of becoming a policeman could have social repercussions. Most of Robert Fuller's London relatives "forbade the very mention of my name in their home after I entered the police service [in 1881], and ever afterwards looked upon me as a leper": R.A. Fuller, *Recollections of a Detective* (London, 1912), p. 21. The main influence on the life and career of the constable was his sergeants, inspectors, and superintendent, all risen from the ranks, men of like education. Promotion was said to rely upon these superior officers, not upon a policeman's arrest or prosecution record.

[48] See H. Shpayer-Markov, "Becoming a Police Detective in Victorian and Edwardian London", *Policing & Society*, vol. 14 (2004), pp. 254, 261-63; Petrow, *Policing Morals*, p. 65. For plain-clothes men, see Leeson, *Lost London*, p. 76; NA, MEPO 2/727; Flynt, "Police Methods", p. 443.

every constable is posted.[49]

What then? For the first leaders of the metropolitan police, Sir Charles Rowan and Sir Richard Mayne, the central mission of the police was the preservation of public order and the prevention of crime. Ten years after the establishment of the force, the 1839 Police Act gave officers extensive legal powers over street activities with its provision of stop-and-search powers. Accordingly, the police order book stated that the police should display "such vigilance and activity, as may render it extremely difficult for any one to commit a crime within that portion of the town under their charge."[50] Policemen were told to know the streets, houses and inhabitants of their beat; they were told to observe the conduct of suspicious persons, and to take notice of those carrying away parcels from a house at unsocial hours. Cases that came before the police magistrates illustrate just how many offenders were caught in the act by virtue of street policing. The police were also instructed to keep a watch on pubs and beer-shops, to keep an eye on beggars and remove the destitute poor, to prevent offences against public morality, such as the solicitation of prostitutes, and to charge persons who were obstructing the street or were publicly violent. In addition to regulating street life and enforcing social rules, policemen were

---

[49] E. Buxton Conway, "Police Life in London", in George Sims, *Living London*, vol. 3 (London, 1901), p. 36.

[50] Wilbur Miller, *Cops and Bobbies. Police Authority in New York and London, 1830-1870* (Chicago, 1977), passim; P.T. Smith, *Policing Victorian London* (Westport, CT, 1985), passim; Shpayer-Makov, *Making*, p. 115, 143; J. Winter, *London's Teeming Streets 1830-1914* (London, 1993), p. 61. In Mark Neocleous's fevered hands, street policing becomes the primum mobile of the project to "confirm the power of capital as the new master": *The Fabrication of Social Order. A Critical Theory of Police Power* (London, 2000), pp, 75-6. And cf. B. Weinberger, *The Best Police in the World. An Oral History of English Policing from the 1930s to the 1960s* (Aldershot, 1995), pp. 161-62. This street policing mission meant that the beat policeman had the discretionary power to ignore a large number of offences or potential offences, or use techniques that fell short of arrest and conveyance to the police station: *Report of the Royal Commission upon the duties of the Metropolitan Police*, PP. 1908 [Cd. 4156], vol. L, p. 101 [hereafter *RC on Metropolitan Police*].

required to provide an array of essential services: seizing stray dogs, helping lost children, taking accident victims to the hospital, admitting the houseless poor to the casual wards, inspecting common lodging houses, and regulating street trading and traffic.[51]

In all, patrol work was the alpha and omega of policing, the goal being to constrain and deter. What has been called the 'scarecrow' function of policing was performed by an active patrolling presence on the streets. By focusing on public order in the city streets, and controlling those activities that were thought to disrupt this order, policemen inevitably dealt largely with costermongers or barrow-boys, casual labourers, vagrants and beggars, drunks, prostitutes, and petty thieves: in short, the economically marginal, those who lived their lives in the street and public places. The presence of uniformed constables was meant to send a message to all potential lawbreakers that they were known and under surveillance, and at risk of being caught in the act.[52]

---

[51] The metropolitan police were employed as assistant relieving officers, so that the houseless poor seeking admission to the casual wards first had to apply for admission at the police station. Other homeless people were moved on from park bench and alleyway, or arrested for sleeping out or begging. Between 1851 and 1894, the police had the inspection of the common lodging houses and their large floating population. In the Whitechapel division in July 1905, there were 4,302 men and 687 women in lodging houses; most were dock labourers, itinerant traders, and newspaper boys, while 500 were vagrants. See H. Shpayer-Makov, "A Portrait of a Novice Constable in the London Metropolitan Police, c. 1900", *Criminal Justice History*, vol. 12 (1991), p. 134; C. Emsley, "'Mother, What *Did* Policemen Do When There Weren't Any Motors?' The Law, the Police and the Regulation of Motor Traffic in England, 1900-1939", *Historical Journal*, vol. 36 (1993), pp. 361-62. For police and common lodging-houses, see *Departmental Committee on Vagrancy*, PP. 1906 [Cd. 2891], evidence of Mulvaney, Superintendent of Whitechapel division, qq. 9631-34.

[52] See Albert Lieck, *Justice and Police in England* (London, 1929), p. 81; F. Bedarida and A. Sutcliffe, "The Street in the Structure and Life of the City: Reflections on Nineteenth-Century London and Paris", *Journal of Urban History*, vol. 6 (1980), p. 393; J. Davis, "From 'Rookeries' to 'Communities': Race, Poverty and Policing in London, 1850-1985", *History Workshop Journal*, Issue 27 (1989), p. 68. Detectives also watched for suspicious

III

We now turn to the evidence to be gleaned from the unpublished notebooks of the police walks, and from Charles Booth's occasional use of this evidence in the published volumes of *Life and Labour*. A number of themes emerge from the police walks. The most insistent theme was the belief among the higher ranks that the police knew the districts where criminals went to earth, the streets and buildings they inhabited, and the types of criminals to be found in these places. These were the areas to which the police would first turn to find suspects and to recover stolen property. Duckworth took very full notes of his police informants' claims.

Hoxton in Shoreditch was accorded pride of place as a criminal district, said by Booth to be "the leading criminal quarter of London, and indeed of all England." He added: "'Wall off Hoxton', it is said, 'and nine-tenths of the criminals of London would be walled off'" — though Booth felt it necessary to divide professional thieves into casuals who lived from day to day, and a much smaller number who planned the big haul. The latter often had training as locksmith or carpenter, and between jobs maintained "a life of apparent respectability." All these men, said Booth, "are generally known to the police", as were the receivers of stolen property.[53] Hoxton was the melting pot for gold and

---

activity in the streets, and commonly caught offenders in the act: *Lloyd's Weekly Newspaper*, 27 Dec. 1896 (Thames Police Court, two 16-year old pickpockets). See also H. Taylor, "Forging the Job: A Crisis of 'Modernization' or Redundancy for the Police in England and Wales, 1900-1939", *British Journal of Criminology*, vol. 39 (1999), pp. 114-18 for non-indictable prosecutions as an index of police activity. Gatrell in "policeman-state", p. 280 (Table 5.1) documents the enormous expansion of arrests and summonses for non-indictable or summary offences between 1861 and 1901. It suggests that the unskilled young man of London's East End had something like a 1 in 6 chance of falling foul of the law. It is unclear, however, how many of the summonses were taken out by people themselves, as distinct from the police, and how many were repeat offenders for, say, the very common offence of drunkenness.

[53] Booth, *Life and Labour*, Religious Influences, vol. 2, p. 111. See also G.R. Sims, *London by Night* (London, 1906), p. 33. Booth finally said that Hoxton

silver filched anywhere in London, and jewelry and watches were hastily "rechristened." Inspector Morgan, a detective at the King's Cross Road police station agreed, though he enlarged the criminal area: "It would be within the mark to say that Hoxton, Clerkenwell & Somerstown include half the criminals not of London only but of the provinces. 'All the best thieves come from London & they will travel any distance.'"[54]

Yet even Hoxton was no undifferentiated "rookery." The most notorious place was said to be Wilmer Gardens, full of lodging and tenement houses, and of thieves, gamblers, prostitutes and bullies, locally known as "Kill-Copper Row."[55] Another place was Huntingdon Street, where a couple of houses were full of notorious characters. As P.C. Ryeland, who had served twenty years in Hoxton, told Duckworth: "'If ever a burglary on a big scale is planned, it is pretty safe to look here.'"[56] The same police informant identified two other criminal areas. Bacchus Walk, to the west of Hoxton High Street, was "the home of a fair proportion of criminals, housebreakers: a type of street almost peculiar to Hoxton: inhabitants neither poor nor rowdy but sportsmen who break the monotony of their ordinary work by an evening's housebreaking." And Whitecross Street, full of Irish

---

(and Haggerston) had recently become renowned for 'belt and pistol' gangs, "bands of boys [aged 14-17], called after this or that street and making themselves the terror of the neighbourhood." The fatal wounding of a girl and the heavy sentence imposed in consequence had put down this new form of juvenile crime for the time being.

[54] Police Walks, B 353, f. 221 (Morgan). See also Walter Southgate, *That's the Way it Was. A Working Class Autobiography 1890-1950* (Oxted, 1982), pp. 36, 86. After talking to P.C. Machell of Old Street subdivision in the Finsbury Division, Duckworth wrote : "Some skill is needed in housebreaking. Knowledge of policeman's beats & patrols & habits of inmates of the warehouse or dwelling into which he means to break: also a considerable amount of pluck. If you are to have any chance of success in recovering the goods stolen you must be on their track at once. He has known things taken in the West end be on sale in his subdivision within 3 hours of having been taken."

[55] See A.S. Jasper, *A Hoxton Childhood* (London, 1971), p. 16; Raphael Samuel, *East End Underworld: Chapters in the Life of Arthur Harding* (London, 1981), p. 13. Harding's family first settled in the Gardens.

[56] Police Walks, B 352, f. 91.

cockneys, was "'[a] rough criminal spot in the midst of most valuable property.'"[57] Ryeland knew of eight or nine men from this street who were in prison.

Many parts of Bethnal Green were also well known to the police. Inspector Pearn told Duckworth that Cornwall Square, near Cornwall Road, "'is vicious & as bad as any place in Bethnal Green; a great source of trouble to the police; haddock curers its inhabitants; many juvenile thieves.'" Strange to tell, the houses were owned by the Metropolitan Police Commissioner, who had made Pearn smile one day "'by sending down to say that his tenants complained of constant row & absence of any police from the neighbourhood.'" Close by was Warley Street, where carmen and porters lived two and three families to a house, along with some thieves. The latter, said Pearn, "'don't always choose the worse streets to live in; they think they escape notice if they choose a fairly respectable street.'"[58] Further south west, at each side of Brady Street, Inspector Barker claimed that the "thieves & rough class generally 'will do anything from thieving & housebreaking to shooting a policeman.'" There were also a large number of juvenile thieves in the neighbourhood "especially young Jews; they are more cunning than the English.'" In a final sweeping judgment, Barker told Duckworth that when it came to adult thieves, Bethnal Green was (with Hoxton and Haggerston) "one of the districts to which the police turn most naturally for the discovery of offenders & stolen goods."[59]

There were other notorious areas to the south of Bethnal Green, in St. Georges-in-the-East, Stepney, and Limehouse. In St. Georges-in-the-East, close to Cable Street and Prince's Square just north of the London Docks, was Mayfield Buildings, a place of thieves and prostitutes. "Not one male in the street above school age", said Inspector Reid, "that has not been convicted."[60]

[57] Police Walks, B 352, ff. 117, 229.
[58] Police Walks, B 350, ff. 23, 27.
[59] Police Walks, B 351, f. 247; B 352, f. 63.
[60] Police Walks, B 351, f. 19. Leeson, *Lost London*, p. 23, said his first billet was at Prince's Square, close to Shovel Alley, an ill-lit court of 20 houses, inhabited by "coalies" who killed people with their shovels. W. Goldman,

In Stepney, Ernest Street, near the People's Palace, was singled
out by a police sergeant as the worst street in the subdivision
because of the number of thieves and ticket of leave men living
there. "'As bad as Donkey Row'," said Inspector Drew. In
Limehouse, between the Regent's Canal and the Commercial Gas
Works was the Carr Street area known as 'Donkey Row.' The
inhabitants were costers, fish curers and dockers and gasworkers.
Some had been displaced from the courts in Whitechapel and
Shoreditch. According to Drew, the corner of Carr and Elsa
Streets was renowned for gambling; "thieves scattered about but
not a regular thieves colony."[61] To the south east was Chusan
Place, next to the Limehouse Cut canal. "'I don't expect you will
find it in your map, practically only the police know of its
existence'," said Inspector Carter. Duckworth took up the story.
"This is a favourite thieves' resort. You are robbed in the West
India Dock Road: off goes the thief down Chusan street; you
follow & if you are close enough behind him you manage to land
yourself in Chusan Place. There he suddenly disappears. ... As a
rule the thief will have nipped over the wall & on to the towing
path ..."[62]

Moving further eastwards into Poplar, finally, three areas
were known to the police. In the North, on the border with
Bethnal Green, the streets lying between Roman Road and Old
Ford Road was, said Duckworth (on the information of Inspector
Carter), "a noted resort for housebreakers; who are generally men
of intelligence & capable workmen: often they are skilled
carpenters or mechanics."[63] Old Ford was also the resort of
receivers or fences. Second, moving to the far east of Poplar, the

---

East End My Cradle (London, n.d.), p. 50, writes of the pimps, prostitutes,
and criminals of the Alley: "Our parents were continually forbidding us to go
there."

[61] Police Walks, B 350, ff. 61, 149. Booth, *Life and Labour*, Religious
Influences, vol. 1, p. 52, wrote of the Carr St. area: "A social pressure of
great importance in support of order is unquestionably exercised; but the
main representatives of this pressure are the police."

[62] Police Walks, B 346, ff. 89, 91; Booth Collection, Notebooks on the
Religious Influences Series, A 33 (i), f. 50 (Chusan Place).

[63] Police Walks, B 346, f. 71.

'Orchard House' area, a tongue of land surrounded by Bow Creek, close to the East India Docks, where the men lived by casual dock work and unloading barges (since the main iron works and oil mills would not employ them) and the women worked in the factories on the banks of the river Lea, and where the ground landlords were the Ecclesiastical Commissioners, was, according to Booth, "a sort of Alsatia for dock thieves. ..." His main informant was headmistress of the Orchard Place Board School, who said: "The place has been and still is to a great extent a sort of Alsatia: the people seem to be by nature piratical and predatory: here the law scarcely runs."[64] Third, to the far south, on the Isle of Dogs, an isthmus in the Thames, and "an island of Docks" (the West India and the Milwall docks), where a close-knit and isolated working-class people resided, the chief vices were said by Inspector Carter to be drinking and gambling and thieving. The latter was confined to boys who purloined old iron and goods from leaky sacks "as a sign of prowess" and from a "love of mischief;" "certain it is", said Carter, "that the Island provides more juvenile thieves than any other portion of the K Police Division."[65]

Duckworth's police informants also revealed their intimate knowledge of the forced migration of those they policed. The most disreputable criminal ghetto in Bethnal Green was the Old Nichol, bounded by High Street, Shoreditch, and Hackney Road to the north, and Spitalfields to the south, the principal streets of which were Boundary Street, Old Nichol Street, The Mount, and Church Street. Artisans (cabinet makers, chair makers, shoemakers), hawkers, dealers, and casual labourers shared the housing in this quarter. Charles Booth stated: "for brutality within the circle of family life, perhaps nothing in all

---

[64] Booth Collection, Notebooks on the Religious Influences Series, A 33 (i), ff. 17-18 (Secretary's Report on Poplar & Limehouse); Booth, *Life and Labour*, Religious Influences, vol. 1, p. 50; Booth Collection, Notebooks on the Religious Influences Series, B 174, f. 3 (Mrs. Brown).

[65] Police Walks, B 346, f. 21; Booth Collection, Notebooks on the Religious Influences Series, A 33(i), ff. 1-4, 14 (Secretary's Report on Poplar & Limehouse).

London quite equaled the old Nichol Street neighbourhood."[66] An 1896 London County Council (LCC) pamphlet claimed that no fewer than 64 ticket-of-leave men lived in Old Nichol Street alone. Starting in 1890, however, the LCC cleared this entire area for the Boundary Street Estate, displacing 6,000 slum-dwellers. New accommodation was built for 5,500, but fewer than five per cent of the original inhabitants could afford to return to the new blocks of flats. The majority moved into surrounding streets and quarters.[67]

Inspector Miller, who had served in Bethnal Green between 1891 and 1895, informed Duckworth that the burglars had moved off to Hoxton and Whitechapel.[68] Sergeant French said that the Nichol gang - "thieves, prostitutes, bullies" - had moved from Boundary Street into nearby Ducal Street, Newling Street, Chambord Street, Gibraltar Walk, and Gibraltar Gardens, all to the east of Brick Lane. The whole, said French, was "a hotbed of thieves." To the south of the Boundary Street area, French identified Chance Row, Sclater Street and Bacon Street as receiving former inhabitants of Old Nichol Street. Chance Row was, he said, "'the most noted thieves resort in London; we could but we do not often take them there." On Sundays, they gathered there from all parts of London. Close by was Church Road, where the fish and furniture shops were receivers of stolen property. Sclater Street was the scene of the famous Sunday morning bird fair, and home to a "'rough class, all thieves or receivers of stolen goods; they go out "dipping" on Sunday

---

[66] Booth, *Life and Labour*, Religious Influences, vol. 2, p. 67. Novelist Arthur Morrison immortalized its decaying courts and alleys as *The Jago*; the Reverend Osborne Jay described its street life in *Life in Darkest England* (London, 1891); Arthur Harding's early childhood was spent there.

[67] LCC, *A Description of the Boundary Street Scheme*, cited in "Booth and Social Investigation", Open University Study Guide. The Boundary Street Estate was the first scheme of the newly created LCC. It began in 1890, with the clearance of thirteen acres of slums; the first new buildings were available by 1895; and the estate was completed in 1900.

[68] Police Walks, B 355, f. 181. Miller added that the number of first class burglars was very small; a good man has been a carpenter, blacksmith or locksmith, but by far the greater number have not: "You can see that by the bungling way in which most burglaries are managed."

morning, what we call larceny from the person'," said French.[69]

Booth later wrote that those who lived in the triangle between Sclater Street and Bethnal Green Road – "a rough class of costers, thieves, prostitutes" - were "a very sporting set who live as a happy family, and 'whip round' to make up a purse for bail or for defence of anyone 'in trouble.'" Here crime did not assume "its blackest aspect", the worst form it took being "prostitution carried on with intent to rob, a drunken man becoming the easy prey of a woman and her bully."[70] Further East along the Bethnal Green Road were Gales Gardens, Pitt Street and Parliament Street. The Rev. Lawley, former rector of St. Andrews, said they were the worst streets in the parish, full of "rough thieves." The Boundary Street clearances had stymied any "betterment", since "some of the roughest characters" had moved into these streets.[71]

The Boundary Street Estate was only one such slum clearance scheme in these late Victorian years. In Whitechapel, few areas could rival Flower and Dean Street and Thrawl Street. Crime was still so prevalent in 1898 that the Spitalfields Vestry petitioned the Commissioner of Police for an increased police presence. By then, however, the "reclamation" of the area by the destruction of many lodging houses between 1880 and 1890, and the construction of the Lolesworth and Rothschild Buildings, had the result, said H. Llewellyn Smith, "of causing part of the semi-criminal class ... to transfer their haunts, and with them the supremacy in evil repute, across Commercial Street to Dorset Street and its surrounding alleys."[72] Dorset Street, said Detective

---

[69] Police Walks, B 351, ff. 159-199. Harding pointed to the tenement houses known as "The Buildings" in Gibraltar Gardens: "there were always fights going on there, and the police gave the inhabitants a wide berth — they had a very bad character, and the people in the rest of the Gardens did not mix with them": Samuel, *East End Underworld*, p. 85. Duckworth described the Sclater Street area as "a remnant of old London with ante Board School traditions & habits. French said the majority of them wd not know how to write their own names" (f. 177).

[70] Booth, *Life and Labour*, Religious Influences, vol. 2, p. 98.

[71] Police Walks, B 350, f. 135.

[72] J. White, *Rothschild Buildings* (London, 1980), p. 128; Booth, *Life and*

Leeson years later, was known to locals as "the do as you please", and it was asking for trouble to go there looking for anything or anybody. It was "the blackest of all black spots in the whole of the Whitechapel district", according to Aves. The police notebooks confirmed these judgments. The street was said to be largely one of common lodging houses, full of thieves, prostitutes, and bullies. Young thieves were taught in the kitchens of the lodging houses. Superintendent Mulvaney, head of the Whitechapel division, told Duckworth in January 1898: "'3 stabbing cases & one murder from this street in the last 3 months.'" Inspector Miller laid it on even thicker. It was the worst street for poverty, misery and vice in all London: "A cesspool into which had sunk the foulest & most degraded... Dorset Street might be stirred but its filth wd. always sink again in the same spot."[73]

Another prominent theme within the police notes was the description of pockets of poverty-stricken, semi-criminal, casual workers, which the police entered at their peril. When it came to these so-called "rough" districts, the cockney Irish were singled out, as was the district known as "Fenian Barracks." Furze, Hawgood, Eastward, Box and Gale Streets, a secluded area approachable only from Devons Road, near the Limehouse Cut, was an area of dock, canal and gas workers, costermongers, and female matchbox-makers. Inspector Carter's judgment pulled no punches: "Three policemen wounded there last week. This block

Labour, Poverty, vol. 3, p. 80: H. Llewellyn Smith, "Influx of Population (East London)."

[73] Leeson, *Lost London*, p. 82; Booth Collection, Notebooks on the Religious Influences Series, A 39(8), f. 17 (Aves's Report on Whitechapel). Aves said Dorset St. was the blackest spot, "in spite of the fact that it is being gradually encircled by Jewish quarters ..." Ernest Aves worked extensively on the seven volumes of the Religious Influences Series. From 1886, and for the next eleven years, he was a resident at Toynbee Hall, the East End university settlement: see Bales, "Lives and Labours", p. 121. See also Police Walks, B 350, f. 51 (Mulvaney); B 355, f. 185 (Miller). See also Fiona Rule, *The Worst Street in London* (Hersham, 2009), pp. 68-9, 167. Whitechapel was known, finally, for "van-dragging", the goods removed from passing carts, taken to receivers, and shipped to Antwerp and Hamburg: Police Walks, B 353, f. 223 (Detective Inspector Morgan, G Division).

sends more police to hospital than any other in London. 'Men are not human' they are wild beasts. You take a man or a woman, a rescue is always organized. They fling brick bats, iron, anything they can lay their hands on. ... Not an Englishman or a Scotchman wd. live among them." Carter added: "A cry of police brings help from every house. The inhabitants hustle the police, they organize rescues; not the least bit of good anything less than 6 constables going down in case of a row if there is any prospect of having to haul off any one to the police station." According to Rev. Hazzard, a Baptist minister of a chapel in Devons Road, the people constantly drink and quarrel, but "are not criminal although of course there are some criminals amongst them." Mrs. Davis of the North East Gospel Mission claimed the police were wary of the young adults in these streets "who are most mischievous and they go about in companies."[74] To the south of the Fenian Barracks, between the East India Dock Road and the Thames, were Sophia and Rook Streets, many of whose inhabitants were casual dockers, "a regular Irish den", according to Inspector Carter, "all the vices of the Irish rampant, murder, rows, dirt."[75]

The police pointed out three more rough Irish areas in St. Georges-in-the-East, Wapping, and Spitalfields. North of the London Docks, Pell and Pennington Streets housed a number of cockney Irish, who caused trouble to the police only during funeral wakes, according to Inspector Reid. They were quarrelsome, "'but they fight it out at home & don't give us trouble.'" Reid also said "'for months they are quiet & since dock labour has been more regular the tone & behaviour of the people is quieter than it used to be.'"[76] The rough quarters in Wapping were Upperwell Street, Lowder Street and Love Lane, "very rough & dangerous places for policemen; to be compared to

---

[74] Police Walks, B 346, f. 32-33; 57-59 (Carter); B 176, f. 17 (Hazzard). See also Booth, *Life and Labour*, Religious Influences, vol. 1, pp. 47-49 (Fenian Barracks).

[75] Police Walks, B 346, f. 99. See also Booth Collection, Notebooks on the Religious Influences Series, A 33(i), f. 25 (Secretary's Report on Poplar & Limehouse).

[76] Police Walks, B 351, ff. 15, 23.

Donkey Row."[77] In Spitalfields, south of Hanbury Street, King Edward Street was the home of Irish vestry scavengers, "'a rough place for the police'," said Sergeant French.[78]

In summary, the police informants believed that they were in the know when it came to the criminal and disorderly streets and ghettos of their division.[79] They point out lodging houses where juvenile thieves are said to be trained; the streets where thieves, housebreakers and ticket-of-leave men go to ground; the location of receivers of stolen goods; and the occasional Alsatia where neither criminal law nor police authority prevail.[80] They presume to know the migratory patterns of criminals, especially those displaced by slum clearance schemes. If they give the impression that the number of truly professional burglars and receivers was small, they point to a number of districts that are home to thieves (especially young ones), prostitutes, and former convicts, and they offer a vivid sketch of districts where the Irish cockneys are at their most violent.

---

[77] Police Walks, B 350, f. 229.
[78] Police Walks, B 351, f. 147. See also Booth, *Life and Labour*, Religious Influences, vol. 2, p. 40.
[79] Police attitudes to East End crime and criminals in the Police Walks is, at times, reminiscent of the attitudes ascribed to the police in the mid-Victorian commentary on "the criminal class." See R. McGowen, "Getting to Know the Criminal Class in Nineteenth-Century England", *Nineteenth-Century Contexts*, vol. 14 (1990), pp. 33-54. Narrators like Charles Dickens, who were escorted by policemen and detectives to lodging houses, pubs, dance halls, and thieves' kitchens, emphasized the thoroughgoing knowledge the police had of these places and the extreme deference displayed by their inhabitants: P. Collins, *Dickens and Crime* (Basingstoke, 1994, 3rd ed.), chap. IX.
[80] Inspector Pearn told Duckworth that there were no thieves schools in Bethnal Green because there were very few lodging house. "' It is in the kitchens of the lodgings in Whitechapel that the thieves are taught:'" Police Walks, B 350, f. 11. Pearn also said that in Bethnal Green the main type of crime was theft from tradesmen's carts carrying tea and cheese etc., and that the receivers of stolen goods were the small shops in the neighbourhood: "You cannot convict them 'But if they were not [receivers] how could they afford to sell the tea & cheese they do as cheap as they do sell it?'"

IV

We should be careful, however, not to presume from this evidence that the police gaze was omnipotent. Rather, Duckworth's notes leave the distinct impression that the police intervened in the criminal and rough ghettos only when it became absolutely necessary, preferring to let sleeping dogs lie in the roughest streets. In earlier times, the metropolitan police had been prone to get their licks in first. Superintendent Vedy, who had served in Whitechapel, claimed the police had long been in the habit of taking the law into their own hands: "Many a culprit in the old days got, and preferred – even asked for – 'a good hiding' to being locked up. It was rough justice, often not adequate, but it saved trouble." This was preface, however, to Vedy declaring that the risk of a counter charge meant the police no longer acted in this way. "The result is that they won't thresh (sic) or knock people about on their own sense of what might answer the merits of the case as they would in days gone by. The whole attitude of the police towards street noises and street rows is altered. In the past they could use their belt and did so."[81]

It is not alone a less brutal form of policing that is on display, however. It is more that the police were following an express policy of doing too little rather than too much, a policy that is perhaps best encapsulated as a surreptitious watching brief. The policy was expressed in January 1898 by no less a mortal than the Police Commissioner, Sir Edward Bradford. He was on horseback, making a surprise visit to Stepney, when he bumped into Duckworth. The latter's account of the ensuing conversation is worth quoting at length:

---

[81] Police Walks, B 356, f. 171. See also Divall, *Scoundrels*, p. 17. Some informants still thought the police were too rough and brutal in their treatment of the poor: Booth Collection, Notebooks on the Religious Influences Series, B 173, f. 125 (Sharpe, Secretary, Stepney Charity Organization Society); Timewell, *The Police and the Public* (London, 1898), p. 3; Clapson and Emsley, "Street, Beat", p. 123. For Hugh Gamon the "overweening insolence" on the part of the police was "at the bottom of a large number of the police assaults": Gamon, *London Police Court*, p. 25.

– said that he hoped I found the police had a good knowledge of the inhabitants in each street 'for that I believe is the real way in which they should do their work.' He said he tried to impress on them not to ask questions but to observe the comings and goings of all those in their districts. In rough streets he liked them to know the names & occupations of every inhabitant. 'Then if there is any trouble you can put your finger on it at once & often as not check it before its outbreak by the mere feeling that in some way or other the police do know about all the goings on in a rough district.' The difficulty, he said, lay in preventing the people feeling they were watched: for this reason it was always preferable to do too little rather than too much. ... To be always in the background except when there was real need & then to come down like a thunderbolt was he believed the real policy of the police, ending with 'Don't you think so.'[82]

This policy was evidently adopted at ground level. Duckworth's report on Hackney Wick declared that the police "take the line of no excessive interference with disorder of a mild character: we are told that ... they as far as possible keep out of the way of ordinary street rows, and they themselves admit that they do not go much into a street or district which is too rough: in fact they pursue the no doubt wise policy of not attempting to force upon a district a standard of

---

[82] Police Walks, B 350, ff.180-81, Jan. 1898. Bradford had been a soldier and police administrator in India until 1887; he then joined the India Office before becoming chief commissioner in 1890. Inspector Mason of the Islington Division echoed his approach: "The great thing is to know your rough characters — 'If they know they are known it takes all the fight out of them:'" Police Walks, B 348, f. 115. Superintendent Vedy underlined the 'too little rather than too much' part of Bradford's admonition. In London, said Vedy: "It has always been 'a point of honor' with the Met police to arrest a thief, but, while in the provinces a man has to do something from time to time to show that he is not asleep, in London it has been rather the policy to let everything that could go without a charge do so": Police Walks, B 356, f. 167.

conduct for which it is morally unripe."[83] P.C. Zenthon said of the rough courts around King's Cross Station: "'We very rarely go into them.'" At first he had said, "'We never go into them.'"[84] The Roman Catholic clergy in Poplar were of the view that the police did not do enough, that "they have little power in quelling rows", and that they were never seen except in the main thoroughfares.[85] Finally, the Alsatias were off the beaten track for the police. In the Orchard House area of Bow Creek, Inspector Carter stated: "'a long way for us to come, we do not often look in;'" the headmistress of the Board School insisted that "the place can never be orderly till a constable is stationed there; but at present the police are really afraid to come. The result is that in spite of their thefts (from the docks and wharves) and their disorder few of the inhabitants ever get landed in gaol." Duckworth's synthesis added: "The law as ordinarily understood hardly runs ... & a policeman is very rarely seen;" and Booth concluded of this Alsatia for dock thieves: "It is so remote that a policeman is seldom seen in it, and twenty-five minutes would be needed to fetch one from Poplar."[86] Booth concluded that from East

---

[83] Booth Collection, Notebooks on the Religious Influences Series, A35 (i), f. 71. See also Police Walks, B 346, f. 173: "Of Hackney Wick itself [Inspector] Fitzgerald said: 'It's so rough we don't go down there often.'"

[84] Police Walks, B 353, f. 175. Indignation at the Jack-the-Ripper murders led Samuel Barnett, of St. Jude's Vicarage, to call for more efficient police supervision. "In criminal haunts a licence has been allowed ... Rows, fights, and thefts have been permitted ..." The Home Office, complained Barnett, "has never authorized the employment of sufficient force to keep decent order inside the criminal quarters": *Times*, 19 September 1888, p. 3 (Barnett's letter). Police impotence inspired a rising tide of public indignation: J. Walkowitz, "Jack the Ripper and the Myth of Male Violence", *Feminist Studies*, vol. 8 (1982), p. 556. See also Henrietta Barnett, "East London and Crime", *National Review*, No. 70 (1888), p. 440; Tri Tran, "La Criminalite a Londres au XIX Siecle: Le Cas des Cambriolages Chez Les Particuliers", *Cahiers Victoriens et Edouardiens*, No. 61 (2005), p. 81.

[85] Booth Collection, Notebooks, B 180, f. 39 (Father Thompson, Bow Common Lane), f. 53 (Father Egglemeers, West Ferry Road, Isle of Dogs), f. 65 (Father Lawless, Poplar East).

[86] Police Walks, B 346, f. 13 (Carter); Booth Collection, Notebooks on the Religious Influences Series, B 174, f. 3 (Mrs. Brown); Notebooks, A 33 (i), f. 19 (Secretary's Report on Poplar & Limehouse); Booth, *Life and Labour*, Religious Influences, vol. 1, p. 50. See also, A. August, "A culture of consolation? Rethinking politics in working-class London, 1870-1914",

London they had heard: "As to ordinary street rows and fights … 'the police don't as a rule see them, and don't want to; for one man to stop a fight is an exceedingly difficult task, and to keep real order in such a district as this would require a small army of police.'" "On the whole", said Booth, "it is the policy of the London police to be too easy rather than too exacting."[87]

There are echoes of the same approach in the more innocuous infringement of street regulations. Inspector Barker brought Duckworth's attention to Goldsmith's Row in Shoreditch, a long shopping street posing as a regular market, "but not officially recognized as such; barrows & stalls allowed by the police to remain so long as they do not congest traffic too much" — though there is a suggestion that the police expected tribute from costermongers for not moving them on.[88] As for the destitute and homeless, the police were not always eager to deal with them or effective in doing so. Whitechapel's Superintendent Mulvaney provided a vivid insight into the policeman's lot. Lodging houses and shelters drew the destitute to the district, though many preferred to sleep out of doors. Only if they were without visible means of subsistence could the police charge

---

Historical Research, vol. 74 (2001), p. 211.

[87] Booth, *Life and Labour*, Final Volume, pp. 133, 137. See also Booth, *Life and Labour*, Religious Influences, vol. 1, pp. 52-3: "Nearly everyone speaks well of the police. Even if some think them not sufficiently a terror to evil doers, it is admitted that the line taken is a matter of policy, and is no doubt dictated from headquarters. At any rate, it is generally assumed that the men are advised not to make trouble." There were other mundane yet important considerations leading to police inaction. Constables were not always encouraged by their superiors to prefer assault charges. "Many a time I have been both kicked and punched and have had my charge of assault declined by the inspector": Leeson, *Lost London*, p. 95. Policemen also disliked writing out reports, and having to appear in court the next morning: Shpayer-Makov, *Making*, p. 74; J. Greenwood, *The Prisoner in the Dock* (London, 1902), p. 11.

[88] Police Walks, B 352, f. 21; *Hansard Parliamentary Debates,* 4th ser., Lords, vol. CVIII, 13 May 1902, col. 5 (Earl Russell); Gamon, *London Police Court*, p. 31. See also, S. Inwood, "Policing London's Morals: The Metropolitan Police and Popular Culture, 1829-1850", *London Journal*, vol. 15 (1990), p. 134 for the view that the police accepted "that street trading, even on a Sunday, was an essential, and largely harmless, part of working-class economy and culture."

them. "[I]f they have a few pence, & they generally have, they can only move them on from door to door. Finally they won't move any further. Police dislike touching the class who do this because they are covered with vermin & won't come to the station without considerable handling. Result, they are left sleeping on the doorsteps."[89]

There is also evidence to the effect that the police and the criminal or semi-criminal culture were curiously symbiotic, a theme broached by East End entrepreneur and petty thief, Arthur Harding, and sociologist Dick Hobbs.[90] The evidence to the Royal Commission on the Metropolitan Police (1906-1908) points to, Gatrell argued, "the ice-berg tip of a longstanding system of wheeling and dealing between police and underworld which had its own unwritten rules and at which command officers had no choice but to connive."[91] Informers were used, favors exchanged, bribes given as a matter of course. Booth's informants conveyed an image of a rule-bound, sporting contest. Sergeant French described the occupants of the triangle formed by Bethnal Green Road, Fullers Road and Sclater Street as "a rough class of costers, thieves, prostitutes, bird fanciers ... All a sporting set of men 'who bear no ill will to the police as long as we take them fairly.'"[92] Detective Inspector Morgan of King's

---

[89] Police Walks, B 350, f. 49. See also *Departmental Committee on Vagrancy*, PP. 1906, [Cd. 2891], qq. 9560-61 (Mulvaney).

[90] Harding, *East End Underworld*, p. 200; Hobbs, *Doing the Business*; Hobbs, "A piece of business: the moral economy of detective work in the East End of London", *British Journal of Sociology*, vol. 42 (1991), pp. 597-608. Harding hated the police as corrupt; at the same time, he recognized that cordial relations with the force were an integral part of underworld life. See also, John Marriott, *Beyond the Tower. A History of East London* (New Haven, 2011), p. 295.

[91] Gatrell, "policeman-state", p. 273. In Joseph Conrad's *The Secret Agent* (Harmondsworth, 1982; first pub. 1907), p. 82, Chief Inspector Heat is said to see thieves as "his fellow-citizens gone wrong because of imperfect education." The mind and instinct of a burglar were the same as those of a police officer: "Both recognize the same conventions, and have a working knowledge of each other's methods and of the routine of their respective trades. They understand each other, which is advantageous to both, and establishes a sort of amenity in their relations." The violent anarchist was a different kettle of fish.

[92] Police Walks, B 351, f. 171. Inspector Miller, who served in the Boundary

Cross Road police station thought the relations of the police with criminals was not unfriendly "'if you take them fair & square.' 'They know it's your business to take them & don't blame you for it' but 'its dangerous to take them in what they call an underhand manner.' " So, too, with the use of informants, known as coppers narks or noses, drawn largely from the ranks of publicans, pawnbrokers and lodging-house keepers, who were said to be crucial to detective work: "informers are plentiful but you must be careful how you use them."[93] It was these comments that led Booth to describe the relations of the small number of first-class burglars with the police in Hoxton and surrounds as "curious, regulated by certain rules of the game, which provide the rough outlines of a code of what is regarded as fair or unfair."[94] Violence was a breach of these rules and a consequence of a breach by either party.

Historians tend to interpret this interdependence as a sign of submission of the criminal fraternity to an ascendant constabulary. "It is the police whose presence most powerfully haunts the book", said Gatrell about Arthur Harding's narrative; "the police were accepted as a necessary and quite local evil … adversaries with little larger apparent purpose than to engage in a complicated and terrorizing game of hide-and-seek with the poor." Or again: "[Harding] never doubted the ability of the police to interfere with his life; their presence haunted and influenced his every action. He knew he was a marked man and that blind eyes could become seeing again."[95] Harding himself spoke of the Leman Street detectives as "villains",

Street Area of Bethnal Green between 1891 and 1895, said, according to Duckworth: "Thinks burgling must be a fine sport. Like poaching all classes & all trades take to it": B 355, f. 183.

[93] Police Walks, B 353, ff. 227, 229. The best informants were pawnbrokers, lodging house keepers, publicans, betting men, and cabmen. See Wensley, *Forty Years*, p. 18; Petrow, *Policing Morals*, p. 68; NA, HO 144/249/A54906 (rewards for informers); J. Davis, "Urban Policing and its Objects. Comparative Themes in England and France in the Second Half of the Nineteenth Century", in C. Emsley and B. Weinberger (eds.), *Policing Western Europe* (Westport, 1991), p. 12.

[94] Booth, *Life and Labour*, Religious Influences, vol. 2, pp. 111-12; Booth, *Life and Labour*, Final Volume, p. 138. See also Meier, *Property Crime*, p. 29.

[95] V. Gatrell, Review of *East End Underworld*, *Criminal Justice History*, vol. III (1982), p. 168; Gatrell, "policeman-state", p. 289.

the recipients of regular bribes and favors.[96] But it would be quite wrong to conclude that the police were effective villains. A lot was bluster, to give the impression that they were in charge of their patch. The statistics on arrest rates for burglaries and robberies point, rather, to the impunity with which serious crimes could be committed. In the late 1870s, for example, in less than 18 per cent of cases inquired into by metropolitan divisional detectives was an arrest made. In 1884 in the metropolitan police district, there were 93 convictions out of a combined total of 331 known burglaries, and 58 convictions from 932 known housebreakings.[97] And the effectiveness with which the metropolitan police kept surveillance of the ex-convict only adds to this impression of police ineptitude.

Repeat or habitual offenders continued to be the objects of police concern, particularly as shorter prison sentences led to their faster return to East End haunts. Yet even here, one is struck most by the tentativeness, indeed ineffectiveness, of police practice. Extended powers of police supervision over released convicts were formalized in the Habitual Criminals Act, 1869, and the Prevention of Crimes Act, 1871. The legislation sought to tighten conditions of supervision for ex-convicts (on a ticket-of-leave), to register all those convicted of crime, and to subject "the criminal classes" to police supervision for seven years after release from prison. Habitual criminals now had to report monthly to the Convict Supervision Office in London or to a police station. All ex-convicts and the larger class subject to police supervision were liable to a year's imprisonment if there were grounds for believing they were "getting their livelihood by dishonest means", or if they were found to be acting suspiciously. Photographic registers were brought to the aid of identification, but they soon proved too bulky for ease of searching, and detectives fell back upon personal recognition to discover whether a prisoner had a criminal record. Remanded prisoners of the entire London district were sent to Holloway prison; three times a week plain-clothes policemen visited the prison to check if there were any known offenders among

---

[96] Samuel, *East End Underworld*, p. 200.

[97] Petrow, "The Rise of the Detective in London, 1869-1914", *Criminal Justice History*, vol. 14 (1993), p. 94; Meier, *Property Crime*, p. 28; Gatrell, "policeman-state", p. 288.

the newly imprisoned.[98]

These laws were meant to impress upon habitual criminals that their every move was watched. Ex-convicts were soon complaining that they were at the mercy of the police, and unable to find or keep honest employment. Ticket-of-leave men were commonly arrested by detectives and charged for neglecting to make their monthly report to the police. Arthur Harding was by no means the only habitual criminal to be imprisoned for a year for being a suspected person, a charge that was difficult to refute.[99] Booth's police informants certainly knew where ticket-of-leave men were to be found – Wheeler Street and Gun Lane in Whitechapel; a Wilkes Street lodging house in Spitalfields – but then every three months they were required to see whether ex-convicts were at the addresses they gave. This was done by a special set of plain-clothes men, not the local constables, but even Colonel Monsell, a chief constable, thought this was "a little hard on them", meaning the ex-convicts. By the 1890s, the police were not allowed to tell employers that they were engaging an ex-convict, "though they used to be", said Inspector Reid of the Leman Street subdivision in Whitechapel, and an exchange between Inspector Thorpe of the Islington division and Duckworth was less than convincing: "'It is a foul libel that the police give information to employers.' Well, but it is sometimes done because I certainly know of at least one case. 'That must have been where the employer asked of the local police whether any of his men were on ticket-of-leave, then it might be done.'" [100]

Arthur Harding was certainly of the view that once you had been convicted, you were fair game and the police could do anything with you. The Prevention of Crimes Act was known in

[98] Petrow, *Policing Morals*, p. 51; Meier, *Property Crime*, p. 32; B. Godfrey, D, Cox, S.D. Farrall, *Serious Offenders. A Historical Study of Habitual Criminals* (Oxford, 2010), pp. 65-68; J. Jager, "Photography a means of surveillance? Judicial photography, 1850-1900", *Crime, History & Societies*, vol. 5 (2001), p. 38.

[99] Samuel, *East End Underworld*, pp. 68, 83, 188.

[100] Police Walks, B 353, f. 213; B 351, ff. 92-3; B 348, f. 7.

the Nichol, where Harding lived, as "the fly-paper": once caught, it was impossible to escape. In his evidence to the Royal Commission upon the Duties of the Metropolitan Police, Harding claimed to have been falsely arrested in September 1906 in connection with a spate of Bethnal Green robberies, and later charged with striking a policeman, "in pursuance of the police policy of continually harassing men who are known to them as having been once or more times convicted." He even suggested that his case threw light "on the gradual process of manufacture of criminals under the present police system in the Metropolis."[101] Predictably, the Royal Commission refused to broaden the enquiry to encompass this charge, and corroboration of such abuses was hardly to be expected from the police themselves. Yet one detective, Inspector Morgan of the Finsbury division, told Booth that "it was very rare now that detectives got up imaginary burglaries etc. to gain kudos for themselves. 'But it *was* done & is still done sometimes.'"[102]

The evidence on the other side of the equation, suggesting that the metropolitan police never secured an effective scrutiny of habitual criminals, is more compelling. For a start, many of Booth's police informants insisted that official rules prevented them from hounding ticket-of-leave men. Superintendent Vedy added: "The best proof of it is that practically none of the uniformed men have any idea of who are ticket men & who are not. Plain clothes men & inspectors are only aware of their names."[103] Other informants insisted that employers were never told they were employing ticket-of-leave men (though just as insistently ex-convicts continued to complain of harassment), and that the police helped offenders to find work.[104] More significantly, the metropolitan magistrates for a

[101] Sarah Wise, *The Blackest Streets* (London, 2009), p. 93; *RC on Metropolitan Police*, PP. 1908 [Cd. 4156], vol. L, p. 330, XII: Case of Arthur Tresardan, Commonly Called Harding.
[102] Police Walks, B 353, f. 225, emphasis in original.
[103] Police Walks, B 349, f. 39.
[104] Police Walks, B 355, f. 191 (Supt. Smith, C Division): "It is to the police interest to get convicts work because they are less trouble when at work than when on the loose." See Booth, *Life and Labour*, Final Volume, p. 138: "On

decade refused to enforce the habitual criminals legislation. In late 1869, Superintendent Howard of the Whitechapel division reported that East London magistrates would not punish a man "merely for being in the streets, although he may be a convicted thief and the well-known associate of bad characters." By 1872, magistrates were blocking the effective supervision of registered habitual criminals by insisting that only the Commissioner of Police in person had the power to enforce supervision and to act against habitual criminals who failed to notify a change of address or for "living dishonestly."[105] Not until 1879, when the law was changed, could police supervision be seriously attempted. Yet not until 1889, were systematic means adopted in the metropolis to enforce supervision and invoke the powers available to the police. Hence, Sir Robert Anderson, the head of the Criminal Investigation Department, declared in 1891 that the habitual criminals legislation was "almost a dead letter;" and the Committee on the Identification of Criminals concluded in 1900 that in London the proportion of habitual criminals who were arrested but who escaped identification was markedly higher than elsewhere.[106] In all, the habitual criminals legislation did little to

---

this point all the police state that no information about ticket-of-leave men is given, and the official rules as to this are very strict." See also Divall, *Scoundrels*, p. 88.

[105] S.J. Stevenson, "The 'habitual criminal' in nineteenth-century England: some observations on the figures", *Urban History Yearbook* (Leicester, 1986), p. 48; C. Emsley, *Crime and Society in England 1750-1900* (Harlow, 2005), p.24. See also *Report of the Departmental Commission appointed by the Secretary of State for the Home Department to inquire into the State, Discipline, and Organisation of the Detective Force of the Metropolitan Police, 1878*, in NA, HO 45/9442/66692. See evidence of Detective Inspector John Shore, Superintendent James Thomson, and Col. James Fraser, Commissioner of the City of London Police. Fraser stated that the police supervision of criminals was "an absolute farce as at present carried on. It is impossible that any criminal sentenced to police supervision for a certain number of years, or who is out on ticket of leave ... can be watched by the police, unless he chooses to be watched."

[106] R. Anderson, "Morality by Act of Parliament", *The Contemporary Review*, vol. 59 (1891), p. 86; J. Holt Schooling, "Crime. Part IV", *The Pall Mall Magazine*, vol. XVI (1898), p. 241. Prison data indicates, however, that in the late Victorian years, those who were imprisoned were, "hard-core, confirmed criminals, in a new sense", drawn overwhelmingly from an

enhance police surveillance of the "criminal class", and little to diminish criminality.[107]

In all, the police walks leave the distinct impression that the police were not at their most effective when it came to the reactive policing of indictable or serious crime, or the surveillance of the more serious and habitual offenders. Instead, they focused on keeping the streets clean of suspicious characters by using summary offences. The bulk of police (and police court) time was taken up with drunks, vagrants, paupers, prostitutes, gamblers, street traders, and very small time thieves. Yet even here the role of the police and the effectiveness of law enforcement are open to question. In fact, the contested, limited, and often impotent nature of London policing emerges most strongly in relation to the morals offences — drinking, prostitution and gambling — that absorbed such an inordinate amount of police time and energy, and about which Booth's police informants were most informative (since Booth wanted to know about the spiritual and moral condition of the population). Indeed, most police arrests and prosecutions involved 'victimless crimes': drunk and disorderly

unskilled and illiterate residuum. The percentage of men previously imprisoned for indictable and summary offences increased from 26% in 1860 to 45% in 1890; for females the figures went from 42% to 63% (due to the large number of prostitutes in female recommitments). This was due in part to the shortening of sentences, giving offenders an earlier chance to re-offend, and to the fact that many more first offenders were being fined than had been the case, but it nonetheless points to a more hardened group of offenders. Likewise, the male prison population was older by 1890 (with one half of prisoners aged 30 and over, up from 37 per cent in 1860), and as illiterate in 1880 as it had been in 1845, with close to one-third of prisoners unable to read or write, despite improved standards of literacy among the general population. This data only served to reinforce the late-century view of habitual criminals as members of a distinct sub-culture, as "a growing stain on our civilization", in the words of the 1895 Departmental Committee on Prisons: Gatrell and Hadden, "Criminal statistics", pp. 378-85 at 379.

[107] See Lawrence Goldman, *Science, Reform, and Politics in Victorian Britain. The Social Science Association 1857-1886* (Cambridge, 2002), pp. 169-70; L. Radzinowicz and R. Hood, *A History of English Criminal Law and its Administration from 1750*, vol 5 (London, 1986), pp. 258-60; T.G. Stanford, "The Metropolitan Police 1850-1914: Targeting, Harassment and the Creation of a Criminal Class", Ph.D. thesis, 2007, University of Huddersfield, pp. 78-79.

offences; and offences under police and vagrancy acts. The police used considerable discretion in whether to arrest, whether to charge, or whether to use informal discipline, releasing without charge after a night in the cells. The policing of morals offences, moreover, took place over wide swathes of the East End, not alone among the rough spots of the region. It is to the policing of these offences that we turn in the following sections.

V

Public houses, said Charles Booth, played a larger part in people's lives than clubs or friendly societies, churches or missions, "or perhaps than all put together", and they were typically orderly places. "Go into any of these houses — the ordinary public-house at the corner of any ordinary East End street — there ... will be perhaps half-a-dozen people, men and women, chatting together over their beer ... The whole scene comfortable, quiet, and orderly."[108] The police guides thought coal porters, dockers and carmen, boot and shoemakers, the building trade, and the furniture trade to be the heaviest drinkers. The furniture trade, said P.C. Ryeland, "keep Saint Monday & 'work a ghost' on Friday night to make it possible." There was a consensus of opinion, according to Booth, that "while there is more drinking there is less drunkenness than formerly, and that the increase in drinking is to be laid mainly to the account of the female sex."[109] Much of this opinion came from the police guides,

---

[108] Booth, *Life and Labour*, Poverty, vol. 1, p. 114. The pub and the school were, said Alec Paterson, "the most frequent landmarks in the landscape." In 1896, there was a pub for every 393 persons in London. The pubs were bright and garish, said Paterson, and men were very "moth-like." See A. Paterson, *Across the Bridges. or Life by the South London River-Side* (London, 1918, first pub. 1911), p, 5. See also E. Ross, *Love and Toil. Motherhood in Outcast London, 1870-1918* (Oxford, 1993), p. 43.

[109] Police Walks, B 352, f. 241; Booth, *Life and Labour*, Final Volume, p. 59. See also Himmelfarb, *Poverty and Compassion*, p. 120; G. Stedman Jones, "Working-class culture and working-class politics in London, 1870-1900: Notes on the remaking of a working class", in idem., *Languages of class* (Cambridge, 1983), p. 198. Duckworth reported that working men in Hackney estimated that they spent one-fifth to one-fourth of their income on

among whom, however, there was a diversity of view. Inspector Barker said that the last two years in Seabright and Viaduct Streets, south of Bethnal Green Road, a center for home cabinet work and weaving, had been very prosperous: "'The people do not save, they spend it all in drink.'" A few streets to the east, in Pott and Pitt Streets were a set of people (costers, market bag makers and toyhorse makers) "who worked honestly for their living & got drunk on Saturday nights but are not troublesome to the police." Yet Inspector Pearn described Usk Street, off Green Street, in Bethnal Green as "'working class but quite 9/10ths of them have been at the station for drunkenness." Barker also accepted that: "The amount of drunkenness is still a sure sign of the amount of work in Bethnal Green so that 'we are busiest when the people are most prosperous.'"[110]

Clergymen from Limehouse, Poplar and the Isle of Dogs agreed that there had been a great outbreak of drink in 1897, as trade and prosperity improved, as the temperance movement collapsed, and as the Jubilee provided an occasion for excess. Booth expanded on this by saying that the winter of 1896-97 had seen such great prosperity that 'slate clubs' paid out large sums at Christmas: "much undoubtedly went in drink, and we have been told by many informants that never before have they been witnesses to such scenes of drunkenness."[111] The police guides also described a sturdy female pub culture, particularly on Mondays, when the clothes were back in pawn and the rent paid.

_____

drink; the average respectable worker earning 25 shillings spent five or six shillings on beer and tobacco: Booth Collection, Notebooks on the Religious Influences Series, A 35(i), ff. 74-5.

[110] Police Walks, B 351, ff. 215, 221; B 352, f. 15 (Barker); B 350, f. 23 (Pearn); Booth, *Life and Labour*, Religious Influences, vol. 2, p. 96.

[111] Booth Collection, Notebooks on the Religious Influences Series, B 169 (Rev. Chandler, Poplar; Rev. Cowan, Isle of Dogs; Rev. Gurdon, Limehouse; Rev. Beardall, Poplar); B 170, f. 55 (Mr. Neil, Poplar); Booth, *Life and Labour*, Religious Influences, vol. 1, p. 12. The *Toynbee Record* added that Christmas 1898 "has been one of the most drunken on record": *The Toynbee Record*, Feb. 1899, p. 70. In Bethnal Green, Saint Monday was generally observed, but the worst times were Bank holidays. "Bootmakers and cabinet makers observe the feast for a week", said Barker: Police Walks, B 352, f. 63.

In Ida Street, in Bromley, north of the East India Dock Road, according to Inspector Carter, "Monday is recognized as ladies' day: in Carr Street [Donkey Row] it is known as 'cowshed' day & probably here also; poor women being known to their husbands & male neighbours as 'cows.' " Superintendent Mulvaney thought the increase of female drinking had led to a greater incidence of drunkenness among women than men in Whitechapel, and Inspector Weidner added: "the traditional disgrace attaching to women's drunkenness has been destroyed." Booth concluded that this was "one of the results of the emancipation of women and of her increasing financial independence."[112]

As for the law, before 1902 the police had no power to arrest persons who were drunk and incapable. Persons found drunk in the streets were either told to go home (if they could manage it themselves or with the help of a friend), or were taken to the station. There they were charged with being drunk, and when sober their own recognizance was taken and they were admitted to bail. The police had no legal right to do this, however, and they could not enforce the recognizance if the offender failed to appear at the police court, which was true of perhaps one-third of those charged. If the offender did not appear, a summons for his arrest was issued, but if he had given a false name and address, the police had no means of tracing him. If at any point, the drunk became disorderly, the police had a power of arrest for drunken and disorderly conduct. The police could also take proceedings against licensed persons for permitting drunkenness on their premises, or for selling liquor to a drunken person.[113]

[112] Police Walks, B 346, f. 41 (Carter); B 350, f. 47 (Mulvaney); B 355, f. 145 (Weidner); Booth, *Life and Labour*, Religious Influences Series, vol. 1, p. 54; *Life and Labour*, Final Volume, pp. 59, 62-3. See also E. Ross, "Survival Networks: Women's Neighbourhood Sharing in London Before World War 1", *History Workshop*, Issue 15 (1983), p. 10; D. Wright and C. Chorniawry, "Women and Drink in Edwardian England", *Historical Papers*, (Montreal, 1985), pp. 119-20, 128.

[113] *Commissioner of Police of Metropolis for 1880,* PP. 1881 [C. 2969], p. 4; *First Report of the Royal Commission on Liquor Licensing Laws*, PP. 1897 [C. 8356], vol. XXXIV, Minutes of Evidence, vol. 1, p. 197, q. 4310; p.

The number of cases of drunkenness that the police dealt with in a year fluctuated a good deal, according to changes in the law and police practice. In the metropolitan police district, the total number of apprehensions was approximately 35,000 in 1878, falling to 20,500 in 1887, before climbing through the 1890s to 56,000 in 1899. The 1902 Licensing Act, which conferred a power to arrest persons who were drunk and incapable, took the figures to 60,000 in 1903, or 8.67 per 1,000, about 35 per cent of which were cases of drunkenness and incapacity, 60 per cent cases of drunk and disorderly conduct. Within the metropolitan police division, according to Gamon, the apprehensions for drunkenness offences accounted for nearly one half of the total number taken into custody, and about one-third of these offences was committed by women (whereas for all offences male apprehensions outnumbered female ones by 3 to 1). In Whitechapel in 1888, 1763 persons (1028 males, 735 females) were apprehended for drunkenness and drunken and disorderly conduct; 3611 (2023 males, 1588 females) in 1897, illustrating the amount of police work devoted to and caused by drunkenness. Booth recognized the discrepancy between his statement that drunkenness was declining and the increase in convictions for drunkenness in London in the late 1890s and early 1900s, explaining the recent increases by Boer War fever and trade prosperity.[114]

199, q. 4382 (Superintendent Smith, C Division); *RC on Metropolitan Police*, PP. 1908 [Cd. 4156], p. 93. See also J. Paget, "The London Police Courts", *Blackwood's Edinburgh Magazine*, vol. CXVIII (1875), p. 380; Leeson, *Lost London*, p. 36.

[114] Petrow, *Policing Morals*, pp. 214-15; Gamon, *London Police Court*, p. 87; M. Williams, *Later Leaves. Being the Further Reminiscences of Montagu Williams* (London, 1891), p. 364; *Report of Commissioner of Police of Metropolis, 1888*, PP. 1889 [C. 5761], vol. XL, p. 37; *Report of Commissioner of Police of Metropolis, 1897*, PP. 1898 [C. 8995], vol. XLVI, p. 61; *RC on Metropolitan Police*, PP. 1908 [Cd. 4260], vol. L, Evidence, vol. II, p. 7, qq. 69, 72-3 (Sir E.R. Henry); Booth, *Life and Labour*, Final Volume, p. 61. Police practice had an inevitable impact on the police courts. For the day of August 18, 1890, in the Worship Street police court (which included a large portion of Whitechapel, Shoreditch, and Bethnal Green), of the 36 charges that came before Montagu Williams, 19 or 53 per cent were for offences resulting from intoxication. Williams himself claimed that every

How, then, did the police act towards drunks and publicans? Booth's police guides confirmed that a man was "almost always allowed to go home without interference even though drunk if he can manage it ... But he must not make too much noise or be disorderly & collect a crowd in doing so. Then you may run your man in for being drunk & get him convicted ..." Bank Holidays were drunken occasions, but this did not necessarily lead to an increase in charges at the police courts, "because on those days the police are more lenient", said Superintendent Vedy, who had served in Whitechapel. "If a man can get home anyhow he is allowed to do so. On an ordinary day the same man would have been run in for a certainty." Yet Vedy also stated: "cases of drunkenness and disorderly conduct have often been habitually dealt with by stopping, moving on etc. if by any possibility these methods could be regarded as sufficient." In short, police enforced the law with discretion, allowing most public drinkers to go free.[115]

There was a similar reluctance to enforce the law against publicans for permitting drunkenness or for selling liquor to a drunken person. The only way in which the law could be enforced was by policemen entering pubs and beerhouses and seeing the offence committed. This had been found so corrupting to the police that they were not allowed to enter a pub except when called to a case of disorder. Also, the constable had to

---

day, except when School Board summonses were taken, drunkenness offences constituted more than half the total charges heard. On Mondays, there could be as many as 70 or 80 'drunks' and 'drunk and disorderlies.' Almost three-quarters (14 of 19) of the offenders before Williams were discharged, the remainder remanded, bound over, fined or imprisoned. Of the two offenders imprisoned, one had also assaulted a policeman and the other had a previous conviction. In the early 1890s, almost half the charges for being drunk and disorderly were met by fines ranging in amount from one shilling to five shillings, the last amount being only one-eighth of the maximum penalty of 40 shillings: Williams, *Round London*, p. 90; W. Besant, *East London* (London, 1901), p. 234; NA, HO 45/9693/A49404/10.

[115] Police Walks, B 347, f. 183 (Flanagan, Dalston, Hackney); B 349, f. 35; B 356, f. 169 (Vedy).

prove the man was drunk and that he had been served while drunk. Inspector Flanagan of Dalston police station in Hackney testified that it was difficult to get evidence that a person had been served while drunk: "Those in the bar at the same time are very unwilling to give it." Inspector Reid took a similar approach. As Duckworth understood him to say: "He wd never accuse the publican of having encouraged drunkenness even tho' he saw a man walk down the street drunk after having been served by him, because he knows that men who are not drunk in the bar become so as soon as they reach the air outside." And Inspector Pearn from Bethnal Green, aware that small beerhouse owners could lose all their customers if they were to evict one, thought it was "rather hard luck on the beerhouse keeper prosecuting him as if he had encouraged drunkenness."[116]

The police blamed the magistrates for the small number of convictions for serving drunken men. Superintendent Weston, chief of J Division (Bethnal Green), explained at length. "It would be much easier to obtain convictions against houses & individuals if the magistrates took a more common sense view of drunkenness." In addition, there was no set rule among magistrates: "Some say the publican must be told not to serve a drunken man & warned by the police as he enters the house, while with others it is enough that the publican has been 'warned' at the time his license is renewed." On top of this, magistrates would not accept the word of a constable that a man was drunk; they insisted upon witnesses. In consequence, "men are only taken up when drunk & disorderly, & disorderliness is the complaint on which they are convicted rather than drunkenness. Hence the police are deprived of the possibility of following up the case against the publican." Inspector Flanagan provided one conclusion: "The constable uses his discretion about running in drunken men and complaints against publicans, a little more on the negative side than perhaps he should do." The law, said Booth less circumspectly, was reported to be "'practically a dead

---

[116] NA, HO 45/9693/A49404/2, Lushington, 26 Oct. 1888; Police Walks, B 347, f. 183 (Flanagan); B 351, f. 89 (Reid); B 349, f. 223 (Pearn).

letter.'"[117]

Policemen avoided charging because of capricious magistrates, and also to avoid losing sleep by having to be in court. The most publicized motive for inaction, however, was bribery: that the police were in the pocket of the publicans. It had been common practice for years for publicans to place pots of ale on sills, "as one would put crumbs for birds", in Gamon's choice words. Chief Commissioner Warren had waged a campaign from 1886 against drinking on duty, which had led to the gradual replacement of beer by money bribes. According to Inspector Weidner of the Tottenham Court Road police station: "At the end of each week the policeman on the beat puts his head in at the pub door, the publican knows what he has come for, he has the money ready & away the policeman goes." He did not believe the offer and acceptance of payments would ever stop.[118]

Duckworth asked every police guide about the practice of receiving either beer or money from publicans. Some police were decidedly uncomfortable when the topic was broached. Most were keen to deny any allegations of corruption, even when pressed by Duckworth: "As to publicans paying the police. Barker said it was never done as the police wd not dare accept the money. I told him I knew that it was done in other subdivisions & that the constant denial of the practise on the part of the police put me in rather a difficult position. He still persisted in saying he knew nothing of it." Sergeant French of the Commercial Street subdivision of Whitechapel said he did not know of "payments made by publicans in place of the beer which they used to get", and Superintendent Weston of Bethnal Green said: "for a

---

[117] Police Walks, B 347, ff. 157, 159 (Weston); B 347, f. 185 (Flanagan); Booth, *Life and Labour*, Final Volume, pp. 104, 106. The following case indicates the difficulty. The police summonsed the landlord of the Duke of Sussex in Haggerston, Shoreditch, for permitting drunkenness. The one drunk the constable saw was not drunk enough, however, to have been charged with being drunk and incapable, so the magistrate of the North London police court dismissed the drunk charge, and in consequence the charge against the landlord fell through: *Hackney Gazette*, 3 Jan. 1898, p. 3.

[118] H. Gamon, *London Police Court*, p. 36; Police Walks, B 347, ff. 191, 193 (Fitzgerald); B 355, ff. 153, 155 (Weidner).

policeman to be served with drink while on duty is a dire offence … for a man to be found drunk practically destroys all chance of his promotion."[119] But Duckworth's suspicions were justified by the testimony of a publican from Burdett Road who described how the system worked:

> He pays the police regularly 1/- per week to the man on the beat. Thinks that all the houses in the neighbourhood whether beer or public pay the same. 'It's not quite our fault that we pay them, they practically insist on it.' Said it was worth being on the right side of the policeman for he cd prevent your getting into trouble in several ways. … when there's a row & you want a policeman he is 'looking the other way', if you have not given him something. He thought the shilling was well spent.[120]

Suffice it to say that clergymen, brewery representatives, and some policemen indicated that publicans gave money or beer to the day and night beats and fixed point constables. In some

---

[119] Police Walks, B 351, f. 247 (Barker); B 351, f. 157 (French); B 347, f. 153 (Weston). In 1882, a Society for Temperance and Christianity had been started among the metropolitan police and some men had become teetotalers: Police Walks, B 356, f. 175 (Vedy). Inspector Thorpe from Stoke Newington said the danger of drinking on duty was such that "whereas 15 years ago not one policeman in 100 was a teetotaler now he put the average proportion as 1 in 5." P.C. Ryeland claimed that 56 of the 203 constables, or better than 1 in 4, in the Hoxton police subdivision were total abstainers: Police Walks, B 348, f. 51 (Thorpe); B 352, f. 111 (Ryeland).

[120] Police Walks, B 350, ff. 239, 241 (Frederick Friend, publican, Lovatt Arms, Burdett Road). Inspector Pearn's evidence concerning call-money paid by publicans was a study in ambiguity, as reported by Duckworth. "'It may exist' he said, 'it may have taken the place of the beer which publicans used to give to the men just before closing time.' Now publicans dare not risk their licenses. Pearn said that even were he to try to stop the practise of giving 'equivalents to a pot of beer per night' he thought he should fail." And Inspector Thorpe of Stoke Newington (to the north of the East End) told Duckworth: "'A crowded district with rough beerhouses is where you will find that the police are offered & accept most.'" There was a large number of beerhouses, the mark of a poor neighbourhood, in Bethnal Green: Police Walks, B 350, f. 35 (Pearn); B 348, f. 39 (Thorpe).

districts, constables who declined to accept money were kept away from lucrative beats lest they 'spoil' them. In others, to ensure the largesse was distributed among the force, no man was allowed to be on one beat for more than a month, and he was not allowed back within twelve months. Moreover, some of the senior ranks (inspectors and superintendents) were still offered testimonials by the Trade when leaving the district or retiring, which could raise sums of £70 or more. Only working men's clubs refused to contribute to testimonials (as they also refused to give beer to constables). Duckworth concluded that there was no doubt the police were "squared by the publicans;" "either in money or kind almost every constable receives something ..."[121]

How far bribery led to the police failing in their duties was difficult for Duckworth to decide: "one witness is of opinion that 'if the police did their duty half the houses in London would lose their license;' this no doubt is to put it much too strongly: but the fact remains that the publicans habitually serve drunken men without prosecution and that the police practically never give a house a bad character at the licensing sessions." Putting it at its lowest, Duckworth suggested, "the connection between police and publican is too close and gives the latter more liberty than is desirable."[122] Nor was it only a matter of overlooking breaches of the licensing laws. Robert Brown of Poplar Wesleyan Methodist Church, South Bromley, complained of police laxness: "Thinks that they are bribed by the publicans ... They seldom take anybody for drunkenness." George Lansbury, a socialist member of the Poplar Board of Guardians, implied that bribery of the police had the expected result: "'In the house at the corner' ... it is a constant thing for a row to happen at closing time; the police come up when it's about over, but no one is ever run in." Booth

---

[121] Police Walks, B 348, f. 77 (Islington publican); B 355, f. 153 (Weidner); *Royal Commission on Liquor Licensing Laws*, First Report PP. 1897 [C. 8356], Evidence, p. 400, qq. 10,400-402 (P. Martineau); Steed testimonial, *East End News*, 8 August 1893, Tower Hamlets Library; Petrow, *Policing Morals*, pp. 200-01; Booth Collection, Notebooks on the Religious Influences Series, A 35(i), f. 71.

[122] Booth Collection, Notebooks on the Religious Influences Series, A 35(i), f. 71.

quoted evidence from adjacent parishes in Bethnal Green to the effect that the police failed to stop street disorder "'and will take no notice of the most bestial drunkenness and the foulest language.'" Inspector Flanagan of Dalston was concerned that the constable who had his two half pints at closing time was brisk enough for a couple of hours, "but after that he gets drowsy he is no longer properly fit." A nurse who had given evidence to Booth believed that whenever there was trouble with a prisoner "the policeman has himself had drink."[123]

One of the East End clergy saw an upside to the bribery: "'It is done more that the men should willingly do their duty than that they should neglect it.'" Publicans treated in order to guarantee help in dealing with drunken men. P.C. Ryeland of Hoxton went further: "'You see we can completely change the character of the trade of a man's house if we want to by moving on the rough customers & shewing them it is no place for them.'" Yet here, too, there is a sense that the police were bribed to turn a blind eye. The proprietor of the Ordnance Tavern, Barking Road, Canning Town, said that the policeman on point duty just outside "if he chose he could run each one of these men in as they came out. 'If the police made a set against you they could ruin you certainly.'" Since he could not help serving drunken men occasionally, he needed the police "to recognize the spirit in which he did his work and therefore not to run them in. 'This is why it is so important to be on the right side of them.'"[124]

---

[123] Booth Collection, Notebooks on the Religious Influences Series, B 171, f. 13-14 (Brown); ibid., B 178, f. 111 (Lansbury); Booth, *Life and Labour*, Final Volume, p. 132; B 347, f. 177 (Flanagan); Booth, ibid., p. 133.

[124] Police Walks, B 350, f. 139 (Rev. Lawley); Booth, *Life and Labour*, Final Volume, p. 134; Police Walks, B 352, f. 151 (Ryeland); B 348, ff. 125, 129 (T.B. Richards).

VI

Prostitutes could not legally be proceeded against simply because they were prostitutes or because they were soliciting; they had to commit a distinct act that was an offence against the law. The enactments that applied to prostitutes in London were the Vagrancy Act of 1824 and the Metropolitan Police Act of 1839. In the first case, the 'common prostitute' had to behave in a riotous or indecent manner in a public place. In the second case, the prostitute had to loiter in a public place for the purpose of prostitution to the annoyance of the inhabitants or passengers. It was on the interpretation of 'annoyance', and the reluctance of magistrates to convict on the evidence of the police alone, that the main difficulty arose. Prior to 1883, it was understood that magistrates required the persons annoyed to come forward, even though most people were too embarrassed to appear in court. In that year, in the context of panic over child prostitution and white slavery and complaints from parish vestries and vigilance societies, Sir James Ingham, chief magistrate, said he and his colleagues would convict without the corroboration of police testimony by the person annoyed.[125]

There followed what has been described as a four-year crusade against prostitution, the number of arrests of alleged prostitutes reaching 6,000 a year in the metropolitan police district, until the wrongful arrest as a common prostitute by P.C. Endacott of Elizabeth Cass, a dressmaker's assistant, in June 1887. In response to the press and public outcry at police tyranny, Chief Commissioner Warren stopped the police from charging these women unless the person annoyed would attend the court. The number of arrests plummeted by over half to 2,800 in 1888. As Inwood aptly put it, with the Whitechapel murders in mind, "the year in which prostitutes were most likely to be murdered, was also the year in which they were least likely to be arrested." However, the problem of prostitution that exercised the official

---

[125] NA, MEPO 2/ 8835; R. Storch, "Police Control of Street Prostitution in Victorian London", in D. Bayley (ed.), *Police and Society* (Beverly Hills, 1977), pp. 52, 55.

mind was less one of the East End, and more of areas like Piccadilly, the Strand, Regent Street, and the Haymarket in the West End.[126]

Two years of confusion followed. In early 1889, Chief Commissioner Monro complained to the Home Office that whichever line of policy the police adopt, "there is invariably a Scylla & Charybdis, into one or other of which they fall, and I cannot feel any surprise at the system of laissez-faire being adopted as on the whole under the circumstances being the safest." Home Office discussion with the Chief Magistrate made it possible for police policy to revert to the pre-Cass position. Constables could arrest where annoyance was witnessed, and magistrates agreed not to decline to act merely because the person solicited did not appear. Post-1889, however, judicial refusals to convict were frequent. Magistrates still differed amongst themselves as to the appearance in court of the person annoyed by the prostitute charged.[127]

In 1901 yet another summit meeting was held between the Chief Magistrate and the Home Secretary, the former giving fresh assurances that his colleagues would convict on police evidence alone. This understanding was reached once more in the context of a vigorous social purity campaign led by the National Vigilance Association and the London Public Morality Council. The upshot was an intensive anti-prostitution campaign for the next five years before the policy again fell foul of another alleged false arrest, the Madame d'Angely case, which in turn prompted the 1906-8 Royal Commission on the Metropolitan Police. Despite the new understanding and increased police activity against prostitutes in the first years of the new century, it seems clear from the evidence given to the Royal Commission that the police did not touch prostitution more than they could help, so

---

[126] MEPO 2/ 8835; Inwood, *City of Cities*, p. 385. See also F. Mort, "Purity, feminism and the state: sexuality and moral politics, 1880-1914", in M. Langan and B. Schwartz (eds.), *Crises in the British State 1880-1930* (London, 1985), p. 213.

[127] NA, MEPO 2/ 209; HO 45/10123/B13517/18 & 34.

great was the risk of making a mistake.[128]

As for brothels, before 1885 the parish vestry had to initiate proceedings upon complaint by ratepayers, though the police could and did help to gather the evidence that proved a house was a brothel. But the vestries were always reluctant to assume the high costs of pursuing brothels. In 1885, the Criminal Law Amendment Act made it possible to prosecute summarily and more cheaply any person "who kept, managed, or assisted in the management of premises used as a brothel, or was the tenant or landlord of such premises." Even then, the vestries dragged their feet. In the fall of 1887, therefore, social crusader Frederick Charrington of the Great Assembly Hall in Mile End Road, whose chief targets were drink and prostitution, went on the offensive, eventually closing down some 200 brothels in Whitechapel, Stepney and Shadwell, rendering prostitutes homeless and forcing them to work in the streets, just prior to the Ripper murders. In the same year, Chief Commissioner Warren gave directions that the police were no longer to help the vestries by watching known brothels. Warren preferred a policy of containment rather than one of repression. Warren's order was countermanded by the Home Secretary, however, and for the rest of the century, the police assisted the vestries, activated by vigilance societies, in the prosecution of brothels, while resisting all proposals to empower the police to initiate prosecutions. Finally, the Vagrancy Amendment Act of 1898 made "living off the earnings of a prostitute", or pimping an offence.[129]

---

[128] E.J. Bristow, *Vice and Vigilance. Purity Movements in Britain since 1700* (Dublin, 1977), p. 165; Lucy Bland, *Banishing the Beast. Sexuality and the Early Feminists* (New York, 1995), p. 109; Storch, op. cit., pp. 63-4; *RC on Metropolitan Police*, Evidence, PP. 1908 [Cd. 4261], vol. LI, p. 1087, q. 45814 (Col. Sir C.E.H. Vincent, former Director of C.I.D.); ibid, p. 1051, q. 45025 (A.R. Cluer, Worship St. police court magistrate).

[129] Bristow, *Vice and Vigilance*, pp. 163, 166; Storch, op. cit., note 5, p. 68; A. Hunt, *Governing Morals. A Social History of Moral Regulation* (Cambridge, 1999), 161. For Charrington, see H. McCleod, *Class and Religion in the Late Victorian City* (London, 1974), p. 117; and Walkowitz, "Jack the Ripper", p. 558. For Warren, see P. Bartley, *Prostitution. Prevention and Reform in England, 1860-1914* (London, 2000), pp. 161-4. For 1898 Act, see Bristow, ibid., p. 169; Petrow, *Policing Morals*, p. 162.

Booth's police guides indicated where prostitution and brothels were to be found in the East End — or not. Bethnal Green, said Inspector Miller, was remarkable for the absence of prostitution. "Of prostitution there is none in Bethnal Green", agreed Inspector Barker; in none of the three music halls would you be solicited. This could not be said of Spitalfields, St. George's-in-the-East, or Limehouse and Poplar. The lowest prostitutes, said Miller, were found in Spitalfields, on the benches round the Church and in the common lodging houses of Dorset Street. Great Pearl Street and Great Garden Street were identical, with the Cambridge Music Hall in Commercial Street a focal point for prostitutes. In St George's, south of Cable Street, was Pennington Street, full of cockney Irish, where, claimed Inspector Reid, "the prostitution is of a sturdy kind and there are no bullies who live off the earnings of the women." North of Cable Street, there were prostitutes, brothels and bullies in Winterton and Planet Streets. Jews were coming into these streets, but Inspector Drew said there were no prostitutes among the Jews. In Limehouse, Rich Street, Gill Street and Jamaica Place, on the south side of the West India Dock Road, were said by Inspector Carter to be "a nest of brothels frequented by common seamen of every nationality." In Poplar, according to Inspector Carter, Flint Street was the living place of prostitutes who worked in the East India Dock Road, their customers the petty officers of ships, their meeting place the Duke of Suffolk public house. Dr. Corner put it more graphically: "Whores in shoals along the E. India Rd by Eastern Hotel." In general, Superintendent Dodd believed that the number of prostitutes had not diminished, but their visibility had. "'When I was a constable in the East End' he said 'I used to see the couples standing two or three deep outside a house waiting for their turn to go in.'"[130]

The police guides also had views on the policing of prostitution. The most strident was Superintendent Vedy: "Before

---

[130] Police Walks, B 355, f. 183 (Miller); B 351, f. 225 (Barker); B 355, f. 185 (Miller); B 351, f. 25 (Reid); B 350, f. 193 (Drew); B 346, f. 81; B 346, f. 39 (Carter); B 173, f. 157 (Corner); B 358, f. 86 (Dodd).

the Endacott-Cass case they strained the law a little and interfered with women who solicited as being 'disorderly persons.' But now the men simply won't do it. Both the public and the Commissioner complain from time to time, but the men won't charge, 'and there's an end of it.'" From the public side, Mr. Neil of St. Matthias, Poplar, confirmed Vedy's opinion. "The police do not touch soliciting. Since the Cass case they have been frightened, & leave it alone." And he implied that the result was an increase of public prostitution in East India Dock Road. Dr. Corner, who lived on the Road, also said the police never interfered if they could avoid it. By contrast to the plethora of evidence concerning bribery by publicans, there was little said about bribery and prostitution. Inspector Flanagan of Dalston said that street-walkers were too poor a class to give anything to the police, but the brothels did.[131]

The East End police also had views on the issues of the prosecution of brothels and prostitution. None were convinced by the campaigns to close down brothels. Inspector Drew believed there were as many prostitutes in the Arbour Square subdivision of Whitechapel as there were before the Charrington crusade along Oxford Street, while many of the brothels had re-established themselves in Shadwell. Likewise in Limehouse, while the Church and Vestry had procured evidence against the brothels supplying the East India and West India Dock Roads, and even secured some convictions, the women simply moved elsewhere "and became a centre of contamination for other streets". "The Vigilance Committee recognized that the fruits of their work were fraught with more harm than good, & so voluntarily dissolved." The police preferred to know where the brothels were. "Better to have them where you can put your finger on them, than in places where you don't know of their existence until they are firmly established" was Carter's view. Inspector Mason, who had served seven years in Shadwell, thought brothels were convenient for the East End

---

[131] Police Walks, B 356, f.173 (Vedy); B 170, f. 47 (Neil); B 173, f. 157 (Corner); B 347, ff. 177, 179 (Flanagan). For bribery, see *RC on Metropolitan Police*, PP. 1908 [Cd. 4156], p. 131: improvement in the streets and the number of convictions of prostitutes for solicitation in recent years "both negative the suggestion of extensive bribery."

police: "bad characters went there & they always knew how & where to put their hand on them."[132]

There was some opinion, finally, in favor of regulation. Vedy accepted that this would mean the licensing and thus the public recognition of morality. "'But why are public houses licensed, except for the purpose of keeping in check what is considered to be a social danger.'" Superintendent Mulvaney said that if there was a demand for brothels there was no point in suppressing them. He was in favor of state inspection and regulation. Licensing, it was thought, would give the police grounds for clearing the streets of prostitutes, and would take business away from the bullies and 'ponces' who were uniformly scorned, even by hardened criminals like Arthur Harding.[133]

VII

The laws against gambling were, to quote the magistrate of Marlborough Street police court, "in a chaotic and ineffective condition." The Lotteries and Betting Act of 1853 suppressed betting shops and made off-course cash betting, practiced widely in working-class districts, illegal. Enforcement of the law, however, came to depend on local by-laws regulating the streets. In London, two statutes were employed against street betting, the Metropolitan Streets Act 1867, under which the police could arrest, "for creating an obstruction in the public thoroughfare", a

---

[132] Police Walks, B 350, f. 79 (Drew); B 346, ff. 81, 83 (Carter); B 348, f. 169 (Mason). See Booth Collection, Notebooks on the Religious Influences Series, A 33(i), ff. 40-41: attempts made to close down brothels in Beccles St., Poplar, "Church & vestry alike recognized the futility of their efforts and desisted." See also S.A. Slater, "Containment: Managing Street Prostitution in London, 1918-1959", *Journal of British Studies*, vol. 49 (2010), pp. 337-38. Cf. S.P. Evans and K. Skinner, *The Ultimate Jack the Ripper Companion* (New York, 2000), p. 472-73, Monro letter, 5 August 1889: clearing out the slums and lodging houses of Whitechapel "would not remove vice, it would only delocalise it, and transfer it to some neighbouring parish …"

[133] Police Walks, B 356, f.173 (Vedy); B 351, ff. 15, 17 (Mulvaney); Samuel, *East End Underworld*, p. 130. See also, Booth, *Life and Labour*, Final Volume, pp. 121-131. See also Petrow, *Policing Morals*, chs. 5 & 6.

bookmaker and three or more clients for street betting. The penalty was a fine of not more than £5. The police were told not to arrest unless there was clear proof of the offence, so they typically summonsed those observed betting. The Vagrancy Act Amendment Act 1873 empowered the police to arrest for street betting beyond the six-mile radius covered by the Metropolitan Streets Act. This Act also made small-scale gaming illegal. In 1898, the London County Council passed a by-law enabling a man to be summonsed and charged if found betting with one other person (rather than the previous minimum of three), which was said to have strengthened the hands of the police. If before 1906, the law was confused and arbitrary, a patchwork of local regulations, from that date the Street Betting Act gave the police a uniform basis for action, making all of-course betting illegal.[134]

Ready money betting and bookmaking took place in streets, alleys, courts, workplaces, shops, and (particularly in the East End) in clubs. Booth counted 115 working-men's clubs in East London and Hackney, 32 of which permitted betting and gambling. Such clubs could be short lived, at the mercy of police raids, but phoenix-like would rise again in the next street. Most were in Shoreditch and Whitechapel; many belonged to Jews and foreigners. Superintendent Vedy thought Jews were especially prone to gambling; in Whitechapel, he said, "the only recreation of the Jew was betting."[135] On the streets, the bookmaker had a 'pitch', one that allowed easy escape into a nearby pub or building, and guarded by scouts whose job was to warn of an approaching copper. The bookmaker or his agent would be there, especially in the dinner-hour (from noon to 2 p. m.), to receive 'slips' from customers, on which were written details of the race, horse, and wager, along with the cash bet. No discussion of 'odds' was required, since the newspapers carried the starting prices. Some sense of the excitement that gambling generated appeared in

---

[134] A. Davies, "The Police and the People. Gambling in Salford, 1900-1939", *Historical Journal*, vol. 34 (1991), p. 88; Petrow, *Policing Morals*, pp. 280-81; note 112, p. 292

[135] Booth, *Life and Labour*, Poverty, vol. 1, pp. 94-5; Police Walks, B 349, f. 43 (Vedy).

Booth's final volume:

> 'See the sudden life in a street after a great race has
> been run and the newspaper is out ... Boys on bicycles
> with reams of pink paper in a cloth bag on their back,
> scorching through the streets, tossing bundles to little
> boys waiting for them at street corners. Off rush the
> little boys shouting at the tops of their voices, doors and
> factory gates open, men and boys tumble out in their
> eagerness to read the latest "speshul" and mark the
> winner.'[136]

From the 1880s onwards, and notably in the 1890s, street
betting and gambling became ubiquitous. Before 1914, probably in
excess of 75 per cent of the working class placed bets on a fairly
regular basis. In addition, the simple coin game of pitch-and-toss
was a widespread form of street gambling, especially for young
men. Attempts to suppress habits of such ubiquity were always
doomed to failure. The police were never likely to convince
punters of the illegality of their behaviour.[137] All this is clearly
evident from the Booth papers and other commentators. The
police guides testified to the fact that: "Betting is increasing by
leaps and bounds, out of all proportion to other forms of vice."
Shoreditch was said to be plagued with Sunday gamblers who
played dice and pitch-and-toss in the vicinity of Essex Street. The
Rev. Free from the Isle of Dogs confirmed that there was "a
tremendous lot of gambling among the boys, not so much on

---

[136] Booth, *Life and Labour*, Final Volume, p. 57.

[137] Mass betting, Ross McKibbin declared, "was the most successful example of
working-class self-help in the modern era. It was at every stage a proletarian
institution ... Although illegal it was almost entirely honest; its corruption
was confined to corrupting the police and it provided few opportunities for
petty or large-scale crime": "Working-class Gambling in Britain,
1880-1939", in idem, *The Ideologies of Class. Social Relations in Britain
1880-1950* (Oxford, 1990), p. 131. Andrew August noted the socialist and
trade union opposition to the prevalence of gambling in working-class
districts, adding: "but they did not recognize the collective defiance involved
in using the streets for this activity in the face of police opposition": "A
culture of consolation", p. 210.

horses as with cards." Pitch-and-toss at the street corners went on all day and every day, Free added, and scouts watched for 'the Copper.' So, too, in Hawgood Street in the Fenian Baracks, Duckworth and Inspector Carter came across a group of men aged 18 to 20 playing pitch and toss. As Duckworth wrote: "Carter surprised at their having let us get so close. 'What were the crows doing?' Crows being those put to watch & keep care." The police guides were also of the view that betting was on the increase, even though it had been driven from the streets (though this was an overly optimistic view). Inspector Reid of Whitechapel agreed that betting had been driven out of the streets by the police "but undoubtedly it goes on where you cannot touch it more than ever." Little went on in the public houses, since publicans feared losing their licence. P.C. Ryeland thought it took place in tobacco shops and barbers; Superintendent Vedy in private houses and courts.[138]

The police guides were especially convinced that betting would never be suppressed by policing. This is Vedy: "If the working man means to bet, police orders won't stop him." Inspector Flanagan echoed the sentiment: "'You must change the people a bit before you'll stop betting ... police orders won't do it.'"[139] The police occasionally tried to act, to judge from the gaming and betting statistics, and of police court proceedings. From 1894, a fairly steady 3,000 to 3,500 people were prosecuted under the Vagrancy Acts for gaming in London. The fines imposed on bookmakers for street betting in the metropolitan police division increased from £2,000 in 1896 to £30,000 in 1905, an increase true also of the Whitechapel, Hackney and Bow police divisions (though with greater fluctuation).[140] It was in these years, too, that CID officers in disguise and (from 1903) plain-clothes

---

[138] Booth, *Life and Labour*, Final Volume, p. 57; R.E. Corder, *Tales Told to the Magistrate* (London, 1925), p. 208; Police Walks, B 170, f. 7 (Free); B 346, f. 33 (Carter); B 351, f. 91 (Reid); B 352, f. 223 (Ryeland); B 349, f. 43 (Vedy).

[139] Police Walks, B 349, f. 43 (Vedy); B 347, f. 181 (Flanagan).

[140] *Judicial Statistics of England and Wales for 1899*, PP. 1901 [Cd. 659, 705], vol. LXXXIX, p. 18; *RC on Metropolitan Police*, PP. 1908 [Cd. 4156], vol. L, Appendix, Return 26, Return showing the Amount of Fines imposed upon Bookmakers for Betting ... within the MPD, 1896-1905.

policemen were increasingly used to attack gambling.[141] As with drink and prostitution cases, magistrates were inconsistent in their interpretation of the law, and commonly required corroborative evidence to confirm police testimony. That thorn in the side of the police force, Mr. Cluer, Worship Street police court magistrate, who gave evidence critical of the police to the 1906-08 Royal Commission, would dismiss gambling cases, for example, if the defendant had no money in his pocket when arrested, on the assumption that he could not gamble without money.[142]

Inspector Thorpe of Stoke Newington best expressed the very futility of policing gambling, especially pitch and toss: "Police have orders to stop it, every now & then they make a raid but the 'crows' at the corner always give warning. 'Besides what's the good of it. with a lot of trouble you may get half a dozen fellows fined 5/-. they pay or go to prison, & then come back & start again.'" It comes as no surprise, then, to hear that the police had to be pressed by headquarters, which received complaints by anonymous letter, to apprehend a certain bookmaker or to watch a particular house. This suggests that the police were largely inactive without prodding. The Rev. Free's complaint about pitch-and-toss included the sentence: "It is difficult for the police to cope with the evil, even when they are anxious to do so, which is not always." Booth quoted another clergyman: "'All must bet. Women as well as men. Bookies stand about and meet men as they come to and from their work. The police take no notice.'"[143]

---

[141] See *Daily News*, 12 June 1897: police raided two betting shops in Limehouse; detectives were disguised as labourers. The seven arrested were to appear in Thames police court; *Hackney Gazette*, 6 July 1898: ten people of both sexes, all aged between 16 and 23, were charged at North London police court with playing pitch and toss. Nine constables had secreted themselves in a covered van from which they jumped.

[142] *RC on Metropolitan Police*, Minutes of Evidence [Cd. 4261], vol. LI, p. 1047, q. 44954 (Cluer); *Hackney Gazette*, 27 April 1898, Worship St. police court case of permitting gaming. Cluer dismissed the case. See also D. Dixon, *From Prohibition to Regulation* (Oxford, 1991), p. 250.

[143] Police Walks, B 348, f. 9 (Thorpe); R. Free, *Seven Years' Hard* (New York, 1905), p. 76. See also M. Clapton, "Gambling, 'the fancy' and Booth's role and reputation as a social investigator", in Englander & O'Day, *Retrieved Riches*, p. 369.

From the futility of policing gambling came the practice of bribery. Duckworth synthesized the attitude of the police in North London in this way: "'It will go on whatever we do: why not then make something out of it for ourselves: it wont harm anybody & it will certainly benefit us.'" Not that the police guides ever went on record. The more revealing testimony came from H.G. Mankin of the North London Club & Institute in Pentonville, though Duckworth thought he might have laid it on a bit thick. The police did not wish to stop betting in the pubs, said Mankin; they even liked a flutter themselves. Every new inspector would launch a raid on gambling clubs, chiefly to be sure of blackmail. Mankin claimed that one gambling club paid the inspector £10 per week to be 'given the wheeze' in advance of a police visit. At some stations, according to Arthur Harding, the police let gambling clubs, especially Jewish 'spielers', remain operative, as conduits that fed information concerning anarchists and socialists to the CID and Special Branch. Even the Royal Commission's Report, while refusing to conclude that bribery was an organized system, and while pointing to the increase in the number of prosecutions for street bookmaking, concluded: "the practice of receiving gratuities from bookmakers has to a certain extent ... prevailed in the Force."[144]

One of the complainants who gave evidence to the Commission, Arthur Harding, had much to say about police corruption later in life. His memoir insisted that one Jimmy Smith, whose beat was around Brick Lane, 'straightened up' the police each month with 'dropsy' — 1/- per day per constable, sergeants and inspectors more — on behalf of all the street bookies. Ritual raids and arrests were part of the deal. Bookmakers or their scouts and runners expected to be arrested, perhaps twice a year, to go to court and pay the fine, which went into the police pension fund. At least this way the police could say they were doing their job. The outcome of all these local conspiracies was that, in David Dixon's judgment, "an unofficial kind of administrative regulation — with

<hr>

[144] Police Walks, B 349, ff. 45-57 (Mankin); Samuel, *East End Underworld*, pp. 178-9; *RC on Metropolitan Police*, PP. 1908 [Cd. 4156], vol. L, pp. 131-32

bribes and fines serving as licence fees and police recognition as registration — grew up because the prohibition formally prescribed by the law was unworkable."[145]

There are many parallels, then, in the police treatment of these different morals offences. The police were reluctant to be drawn into moral crusades against what they felt were natural vices. The police had neither the numbers (especially with high rates of absenteeism due to illness and injury), nor the inclination to be "moral missionaries", to enforce a code of morality by law and policing, to act against what they deemed to be venial and victimless crimes. Public demand for drink, prostitution, and gambling was too enormous for policing to be anything other than an exercise in futility, though one that could sour relations between police and public, and undermine public cooperation concerning more serious matters. The confused state of the law could also deter police from acting, and magistrates were inconsistent, capricious, and obstructive in the administration of justice, discouraging any zeal in prosecuting people for minor offences. The rank and file of the force believed that was wanted was not more men "run in", but magistrates who would convict.[146]

The police retreated into stylized exercises designed to convince the public, and perhaps themselves, that the law was being enforced — as well as keeping the bribes coming from publicans, brothel keepers, and bookies. Corruption was regarded as an acceptable way of negotiating an acceptable everyday

---

[145] Samuel, *East End Underworld*, pp. 176, 180-81; Dixon, op. cit., p. 229; Gamon, *London Police Court*, p. 34. See also R. Hood and K. Joyce, "Three Generations. Oral Testimonies on Crime and Social Change in London's East End", *British Journal of Criminology*, vol. 39 (1999), p. 146.

[146] See D.J.V. Jones, "The New Police, Crime, and People in England and Wales, 1829-1888", *Transactions of the Royal Historical Society*, 5th ser., vol. 33 (1983), p. 161; A.C. Plowden, *Grain or Chaff? The Autobiography of a Police Magistrate* (London, 1903), pp. 333-34. The vicar of a poor parish claimed that magistrates did nothing to encourage the police to keep good order: "if they take people up, excepting for really serious offences, they are generally only snubbed for their pains": Booth, *Life and Labour*, Final Volume, p. 140. See also Booth Collection, Notebooks on the Religious Influences Series, A 35(i), f. 71.

relationship with the public. The policing priority became the containment not eradication of disorder. The police may well have influenced the location and forms of drinking, prostitution, and gambling, but they did little or nothing to suppress these morals offences. The role the police played, in all, was determined by a complex interplay of the criminal law, the conduct of police court magistrates, pressure from social purity groups, public opinion, central police policy, and the operational conduct and occupational culture of the local police.

Some historians, familiar with the policing of morals offences, persist in arguing that despite the deeply negotiated relationship between police and public, despite the customary set of rules and norms regarding the level of arrests and the taking of bribes, there was no doubt about who was in control of the streets. The police, they insist, brooked no challenge over the use of public space. This is not a conclusion consistent with the evidence of the London police walks. Two of Booth's public informants tell a different tale, one that indicates how fragile was the contract between police and public, how dependent it was upon public opinion, and how easily the contract could be ruptured, to the severe detriment of police authority.

The Rev. Gurdon, Rector of Limehouse, wanted more drastic treatment of offences like pitch & toss and other disorderly conduct — "but admitted that public opinion would not support it, & where it had been tried the police became very unpopular & had a bad time of it ... This is curious as showing the uncertain ground law & order occupies." The Rev. Donaldson, vicar of St. Mary's, Hackney Wick, said: "Police practice can only be just a little ahead of the morality of the district. 'In all they do to suppress rowdyness they must have the moral support of the better class of the neighbours if they are to be successful... The police are really wise in acting as they do; they would soon find out how weak they were if they came into conflict with the neighbourhood on a question like this. The people would find it out too & there would be an end of all respect for their authority.' "[147]

[147] Booth Collection, Notebooks on the Religious Influences Series, B 169, ff.

VIII

The previous sections on metropolitan police practice in the 1890s have argued for the hesitancy, the intermittency, even the paucity of policing in London's East End. The evidence presented pours a dose of cold water on the professed success of late Victorian policing in creating a new level of social order. Where then should we turn to explain the increasing tranquility of the capital city? An exclusive focus on policing omits the important dimension of the interaction within East End districts between policing, popular justice, social welfare campaigns, the activities of poor law and school board, and the police courts. Accordingly, the next sections attempt to uncover the role of economic improvement and the disciplines of the wage relationship; of family and neighbourhood in the settling of disputes, and the fragile contract between police and policed as to which behaviours would be ignored and which interrogated; of the constraints on conduct imposed by charitable and state agencies; and of the division of labour between magistrates courts and popular self-regulation. Historians have long called for such work, in the knowledge that the police and courts handled only a fraction of the delinquency in a community. Over a decade ago, Jose Harris advanced the probability that the family, community, and self-governing institutions of working-class life were at least as important as policing in explaining the fall in crime and popular engagement with the law.[148] Yet historians have been slow to tackle this agenda.

We start with improved living standards. Charles Booth's social survey took place at the end of forty years of rapid real wage growth. This was due less to higher wages than to lower retail prices of foods, thanks to increasing imports and lower taxes. London's high housing costs, with rents almost doubling in the East End in the 1890s, kept real wage gains lower than they might have been, and condemned one-fifth of London households

---

107, 109 (Gurdon); Police Walks, B 347, f. 205 (Donaldson). See Booth, *Life and Labour*, Final Volume, p. 141.

[148] J. Harris, *Private Lives, Public Spirit. Britain 1870-1914* (London, 1994), p. 214.

to homes of only one room. Yet, as Dingle argued, between 1880 and 1895, when real wages rose as a result of falling prices (as distinct from a rise in cash wages), the level of drink consumption stagnated, the enhanced purchasing power allowing the housewife to buy more with her fixed budget. Less went on drink; more went to food.[149] Booth's investigators recorded these improvements. Ernest Aves's chapter on the furniture trade recorded an extensive fall in prices in recent years, increasing the real wages of men who nominally earned the same amount as fifteen years ago. His report on Whitechapel, Spitalfields, and St. George's underlined "[t]he upward tendency of wages and, apart from rent, the downward tendency of the expenses of living." The report on Poplar and Limehouse stated that the entire district had experienced prosperity in recent years, in large part because "food & all necessaries are very cheap." Also, work for women in the jam and provision factories had so increased that "the proportion of money earned by women is everywhere on the increase."[150] Of course, the evidence is contradictory, since Booth's people also reported high levels of drink consumption in the later 1890s, but overall improved living standards were probably conducive to less disorder.

What of the disciplines of the wage relationship? Few East End workers were employed in large-scale factory production, so few were subject to the discipline required of factory work. Large numbers worked for themselves or others on a catch-as-catch-can basis — dockers, porters, carters, and costermongers. It is claimed, in consequence, that East End workers developed an independence of mind and behaviour, a quick-witted individualism, and an antipathy to the arbitrary

---

[149] A.E. Dingle, "Drink and Working-Class Living Standards in Britain, 1870-1914", *Economic History Review*, vol. 25 (1972), pp. 617-22.

[150] Aves, "The Furniture Trade", in Booth, *Life and Labour*, Poverty, vol. 4, p. 207; Booth Collection, Notebooks on the Religious Influences Series, A 39(8), f. 11 (Aves' Report on Whitechapel); ibid., A 32(i), f. 10; A 33(i), f. 12b. See also J. White, "Jewish Landlords, Jewish Tenants: An Aspect of Class Struggle Within the Jewish East End, 1881-1914", in Newman (ed.), *The Jewish East End* (London, 1981), p. 208; Ross, *Love and Toil*, pp. 41-2.

imposition of authority.[151] Perhaps in consequence, a high level of workplace crime and a high tolerance of delinquency on the part of employers characterized work relations. For many workers, as August claims, insubordination plus low wages passed seamlessly into theft, "which was endemic in London work places." Employers were willing to absorb a large amount of pilfering, and typically more prepared to use informal sanctions against crime, such as firing the offender, than formal prosecution. This approach was true even of the large dock companies with their own police forces. Dockers caught thieving were prosecuted if an exemplary sentence were thought necessary. Frederick Lawley was sentenced to three months' hard labour for stealing two brass bearings taken from a locomotive crane in the West India dock. The crane and machinery had been considerably plundered during the past three

---

[151] See Hobbs, *Doing the Business*, pp. 21, 97, 116; McKibbin, "Why was there no Marxism in Great Britain", in idem, *Ideologies of Class*, p. 4. Of the 180-190,000 adult working men in the East End in 1891, some 55,000 were in unskilled jobs, including14,000 dock and wharf labourers, 3,500 building labourers, 8,000 carmen and carriers, 6,000 porters, 3,500 gasworkers, 1,500 coal porters and heavers, 1,500 factory labourers, 2,500 warehousemen, and 9,000 'general labourers.' Over half of working men were in skilled, professional, or trading occupations. The main center of the East End furniture trade was in the Curtain Road and Old Street area of Shoreditch, gradually extending into Bethnal Green and Hoxton. Boot and shoe production was also concentrated in Shoreditch and Bethnal Green. The furniture, clothing, and footwork industries responded to provincial competition by extending the sweating and out-work system, with its associated ills of low wages, long hours, and overcrowded work conditions. Marriott says that in 1891 the total engaged in *sweated* trades in East London was 15 per cent of all those employed. In what the Booth survey termed 'Outer East London', comprising the districts of Poplar, Bromley, Bow, Isle of Dogs, Bethnal Green East, and parts of Mile End Old Town, Stepney and Limehouse, contained, said Booth, "a solid English industrial population endowed with noticeable vigour and independence of character …": P. Kirkham et al, *Furnishing the World. The East London Furniture Trade 1830-1980* (London, 1987), p. 15; A. August, *Poor Women's Lives. Gender, Work, and Poverty in Late-Victorian London* (London, 1999), p. 35; D.F. Schloss, "Bootmaking", in Booth, *Life and Labour*, Poverty, vol. 4, pp. 69, 158-62; A. Godley, "Immigrant Entrepreneurs and the Emergence of London's East End as an Industrial District", *London Journal*, vol. 21 (1996), pp. 38-42; M. Brodie, *The Politics of the Poor. The East End of London* (Oxford, 2004), p. 25; Marriott, *Beyond the Tower*, p. 222.

months, endangering those who worked on the machinery. Yet dockers caught thieving in the London docks were frequently reprimanded, cautioned, and suspended for a few days, and neither fired nor prosecuted. Dismissal did not typically lock offenders into a life of crime: there were so many small and medium-sized employers that ex-offenders could always find new jobs.[152]

There is evidence of changes in work and work practices leading to improvements. The riverside labour market was beginning to contract under the impact of mechanization and increased labour productivity, and new docks took the shipping lower down the Thames. As Booth recorded, "the men and their work have to a great extent moved further down the river; and such employment as remains has become more regular in character." Superintendent Mulvaney expressed the opinion that London was less of a port city: "In consequence, fewer sailors, less drunkenness, less prostitution ..." East End magistrate, Montagu Williams, thought Ratcliff Highway had improved as new docks drew shipping lower down the Thames, and liners were manned by a better class of men. Inspector Carter claimed that Limehouse was better for "the facility now given to sailors to send their money home", money formerly spent in pubs and brothels.[153]

The disciplines of organized labour were hardly extensive

[152] August, "A culture of consolation", pp. 213-14; *Lloyd's Weekly Newspaper*, 19 June 1898 (Lawley); Tri Tran, "Les vols dans les docks de Londres au XIX siecle", *Revue Française De Civilisation Britannique*, Vol. XII (2003), pp. 87-89; J. Schneer, *London 1900. The Imperial Metropolis* (New Haven, 1999), pp. 46, 49. See also Davis, "Prosecutions and Their Context", p. 410; Leeson, *Lost London*, p. 147; B. Webb, *My Apprenticeship*, p. 302; B. Potter, "The Docks", in Booth, *Life and Labour*, Poverty, vol. 4, p. 18. Cf. B.S. Godfrey et al, *Criminal Lives. Family Life, Employment, and Offending* (Oxford, 2007), p. 182. For examples of work theft in bus transport (conductors) and milk selling (milk carriers), see Booth, *Life and Labour*, Industry, vol. 3, pp. 179, 311-12.

[153] Booth, *Life and Labour*, Religious Influences Series, vol. 2, p. 4; Police Walks, B 350, f. 47 (Mulvaney); Williams, *Round London*, p. 82; ibid., B 346, ff. 84-5, 145 (Carter). See also P. de Rousiers, *The Labour Question in Britain* (London, 1896), p. 354; M. Ball and D. Sunderland, *An Economic History of London, 1800-1914* (London, 2001), p. 224.

but occasionally in play. London was a poor trade union town. The gains made in the New Unionism of the late 1880s were soon lost in the employers' counter-offensive of the early 1890s. By 1897, only 3.5 per cent of the London population was in trade unions. The East End was no exception. The preponderance of small workshops and domestic work, the numbers of casual and immigrant workers, made labour difficult to organize. The trade unions in cabinet making, bootmaking, and tailoring were small, exclusively metropolitan, and in competition with each other. Now and again, however, there is a hint of organized labour's own brand of discipline. The trade unions in bootmaking, "under which a considerable part of the labour engaged in this industry is organized", according to David Schloss, one of Booth's colleagues, regulated wages and served as provident societies, and "are collectively responsible for the honesty of their members, making good to the employer materials intrusted to a workman and not returned."[154] But such examples are infrequent.

The self-discipline of organized labour was most evident, however, in August 1889 during the Dock Strike when tens of thousands of dockworkers, demanding a pay increase and changes in hiring practices, marched through the London streets with carnival-like floats, and picketed the docks. "The whole history of the world", said The Recorder of London, "did not afford so wonderful an instance of self control on the part of suffering men with starving wives and children, and such discretion and forbearance on the part of the authorities." The police stewarded processions in the city center, allowed meetings to be held at the dock gates, and interfered little with workmen's pickets, despite the pressure to do so from dock employers. Relations between police and strikers remained remarkably harmonious, and few cases of violent intimidation of strikebreakers came before the police courts.[155]

---

[154] T. Olcott, "Dead Centre: The Women's Trade Union Movement in London, 1874-1914", *London Journal*, vol. 2 (1976), p. 33; Jones, "Working-class culture", p. 211; Schloss, "Bootmaking", in Booth, *Life and Labour*, Poverty, vol. 4, p. 125.
[155] Recorder quoted in Marriott, *Beyond the Tower*, p. 192; G. von

Scene from Dock Strike, 1889

IX

Let us turn to the solidarities of the inner-city working-class community. Nostalgia can play havoc with social description when it comes to popular solidarities, so one must try to remain unsentimental. Joanna Bourke has forcefully challenged the

---

Schutze-Gaevernitz, *Social Peace. A Study of the Trade Union Movement in England* (London, 1893), pp. 256-57; NA, MEPO 2/ 226; MEPO 2/ 472. See also, J. Ballhatchet, "The Police and the London Dock Strike of 1889", *History Workshop*, Issue 31 (1991), pp. 57-60. The metropolitan police were more vigorous in curtailing the right of socialists from holding political meetings in public places, such as Dod Street in the East End: J. Lawrence, *Speaking for the People. Party, language and popular politics in England, 1867-1914* (Cambridge, 1998), p. 188. Gillian Cronje argued that the Dock Strike taught the middle class they had nothing to fear from the casual worker, many of whom were respectable and patriotic: *Middle Class Opinion and the 1889 Dock Strike*, Our History pamphlet, 61 (1975), p. 17.

concept of 'community', if by that we mean one "based on reciprocal rights and obligations." She is doubtful whether any real consensus existed in working-class communities. High levels of conflict within these areas suggest that no such consensus existed. She argues instead that the working-class neighbourhood was a contracting society, with individuals bidding for scarce resources.[156] I am not convinced that there is any fundamental contradiction between these two approaches. It is surely the case that the notion of a community with a broad quantum of consensus on some issues can also incorporate the notion of a complex of power relations, especially in relation, say, to the negotiation for the scarce resources of charity and welfare.

It still seems valid, therefore, to ask to what extent did East End communities succeed in regulating their own disputes rather than resort to the police or courts? To what extent did the neighbourhood act as a unit of community control, and as a medium for the transmission of moral standards? Such community- or self-regulation required settled social neighbourhoods where members shared certain assumptions, beliefs and patterns of behaviour; where neighbours felt able to rebuke disorder and incivility; where children were unofficially supervised; and where strangers in the street were closely observed. It so happens that East End communities were both settled and conducive to informal restraints on conduct.

For a start, the spatial conditions were right. A large proportion of the population had been born and brought up in London, and as such had exclusive experience of urban living. Shoreditch, Bethnal Green, and Poplar had by 1911 the highest percentages (in the 80th percentile) of population born in London.[157] Residential stability was high. The Booth team were struck by the comment of Rev. Toye, a Unitarian minister, who

---

[156] J. Bourke, *Working-Class Cultures in Britain 1890-1960* (London, 1994), pp. 137, 139, 150-52. See also R. Colls, "When we lived in communities: working-class culture and its critics", in Colls and R. Rodger (eds.), *Cities of Ideas. Civil Society and Urban Governance in Britain, 1800-2000* (Aldershot, 2004), p. 290.

[157] Davis, *Reforming London*, p. 7.

said of the inhabitants of Elsa Street, Limehouse Fields, a part of 'Donkey Row': "The people cling to the neighbourhood and will not move out. Some have been here a very long time and such regard themselves as the owners of the place and think they can do as they like." Grace Foakes, born in 1901, lived in a tenement flat in Royal Jubilee Buildings. Those on the far side of Dock Bridge would have nothing to do with her side: "They were a community on their own and so were we, although we were all in one parish."[158] Restricted mobility was also influential. Residential change tended to limit itself to neighbouring streets, even in the face of wholesale eviction, so people remained in the same district for long periods of time. Transport arteries (roads, railways, and canals) physically splintered the East End into a large number of self-contained neighbourhoods, heightening community solidarity within these districts. The importance of the neighbourhood as a base for sociability was also underscored by kinship and marriage patterns. In the late Victorian years, in 80 per cent of marriages in working-class areas, both bride and groom came from the same district, sometimes from the same street.[159]

Popular solidarities also rested on mutual help, mutual generosity. As Hobsbawm stated, working-class life was lived "in a

---

[158] Booth Collection, Notebooks on the Religious Influences Series, B 172, ff. 29-30; G. Foakes, *Between High Walls. A London Childhood* (London, 1972), p. 1; D.R. Green, *People of the Rookery. A Pauper Community in Victorian London*, Occasional Paper, no. 26, King's College, London, 1986, pp. 30-31. Beatrice Webb provided an account of two interviews with the School Board Visitor for the Stepney Division, who spoke about the "hereditary casuals" of the docklands area: "They do not migrate out of the district, but they are constantly changing their lodgings: 'They are like the circle of the suicides in Dante's Inferno; they go round and round within a certain area'": *My Apprenticeship*, p. 303.

[159] Dennis, *Cities in Modernity*, pp. 97-98; W. Southgate, *That's the Way it Was. A Working Class Autobiography 1890-1950* (Oxted, 1982), p. 34. Cf. Peter Townsend, SN 4756, Katharine Buildings, 1885-1962, Fieldwork 1957-62, National Social Policy and Social Change Archive, University of Essex Economic and Social Data Service. The use of the word "manor" is a reminder that the East End was originally a collection of tight-knit communities with codes of loyalty.

network of mutual aid and trust largely independent of the law."[160]
Old residents could depend upon neighbours when hardship
struck. Informal exchanges, via kin and neighbourhood networks,
helped families survive illness, childbirth, desertion, or
unemployment. The overwhelming responsibility for social
welfare, especially for infants and children, lay with families and
the neighbourhood. Walter Southgate, born in 1890 near Bethnal
Green, his father a quill-pen maker, his mother a char, considered
that "mutual aid was the keystone of existence when difficult times
came along." Social observers remarked upon the remarkable
extent of goods and services that passed from the poor to the poor.
Some claimed it was significant to the survival of one-third of all
poor households in London. Even Beatrice Webb, unsympathetic
to what she termed the "aborigines of the East End", recorded in
her diary in late 1886: "The bright side of the East End life is the
sociability and generous sharing of small means."[161]

These close-knit communities also enforced codes of
behaviour and respectability. The Rev. Lawley, former vicar of St.
Andrew's, Bethnal Green, told Duckworth that in his parish
"among the very poor there was a strict code of outward decency
which cd not be violated with impunity." He told of a coster who
started co-habiting with a woman who had nursed his wife during
her last illness. "The whole street felt outraged & the pair were
forcibly ejected & had to go & live elsewhere. In this case
cohabitation with the woman during the wife's illness had been
condoned." Booth's report on Bethnal Green noted that marriages

---

[160] E.J. Hobsbawm, "The Formation of British Working-Class Culture", in
idem., *Worlds of Labour* (London, 1984), p. 191.
[161] Ross, "Survival Networks", pp. 6-8, 12-13; idem., *Love and Toil*, p. 134; P.
Johnson, "Private and Public Social Welfare in Britain, 1870-1939", in M.B.
Katz and C. SachBe (eds.), *The Mixed Economy of Social Welfare*
(Baden-Baden, 1996), p. 142; Hood and Joyce, "Three Generations", p. 148;
W. Southgate, *That's the Way it Was,* p. 22; E. Ross, "'Human Communion'
or a Free Lunch. School Dinners in Victorian and Edwardian London", in
J.B. Schneewind (ed.), *Giving. Western Ideas of Philanthropy* (Bloomington,
1996), p. 185; B. Webb, *My Apprenticeship*, p. 283. See also, A. August,
The British Working Class, 1832-1940 (Harlow, 2007), pp. 104-5; B.
Harrison, "Philanthropy and the Victorians", in idem., *Peaceable Kingdom.
Stability and Change in Modern Britain* (Oxford, 1982), p. 221.

were contracted for "pressing reasons" at the last possible moment, "but 'is always intended'; the girls count on it, for the local ethical standard is strong on the necessity of marriage under such circumstances." He was moved by such evidence to conclude that there were "strict rules of propriety, accepted by public opinion, which cannot be violated with impunity by those who wish to live on pleasant terms with their neighbours, though they may not follow the ordinary lines either of legal or religious morality."[162] The rates of illegitimacy bear out the notion of a moral community. East London had a smaller percentage of illegitimate births than London as a whole. While illegitimate births as a percentage of total births were 4 per cent of those born in London in 1890, the figures for St George's, Whitechapel and Stepney were 3%, 2.8%, and 1% respectively. Ten years later, they were 2%, 2.5%, and 0.6% respectively.[163]

Londoners also policed the boundaries of illegality. As Robert Roberts recalled, though "a man might fear the law he feared too the disapproval of his neighbours ..." The pull of what James Robb called "local loyalties" was stronger than the imposition of external rules and authority. Writing of Bethnal Green, Robb observed that a man who stole even a small sum from a neighbour or workmate was chastised more fiercely than one who stole a larger amount from an outsider. George Acorn's Bethnal Green family lived above a woman who dealt in stolen clothes. When the police arrived, Acorn's mother and the landlady hid the stolen property. Yet while these women united against the law, they were not prepared to see thieving as a legitimate form of survival. After the police had gone, the landlady told the dishonest lodger to move out.[164]

---

[162] Police Walks, B 350, ff. 137, 139; Booth, *Life and Labour*, Religious Influences, vol. 2, p. 97. See also G. Foakes, *My Part of the River* (London, 1974), p. 53.

[163] L. Marks, "'The Luckless Waifs and Strays of Humanity': Irish and Jewish Immigrant Unwed Mothers in London, 1870-1939", *Twentieth Century British History*, vol. 3 (1992), pp. 116-17.

[164] R. Roberts, *The Classic Slum* (London, 1971), p. 183, cited in T.R.C. Brydon, "Charles Booth, Charity Control, and the London Churches, 1897-1903, *The Historian*, vol. 68 (2006), p. 502; J.H. Robb, *Working-Class*

Moral boundaries were especially tightly policed when it came to children. Severe overcrowding meant children lived in the streets, and thus were subject to the informal supervision of extended family members and neighbours. Gilda O'Neill, born in Bethnal Green, emphasized the shared supervision of children: "Such a way of life ... allowed you to keep an eye on what the children were up to and let the neighbours police the behaviour of any strangers who 'turned up on the manor.'"[165] Neighbourly surveillance was much more inescapable and effective than that of the police, who had to rely upon witnesses to reconstruct events they typically did not see. The worst crimes against the common law were sexual violence against minors or brutal treatment of children. Neighbours had various courses of action. They might forcibly intervene, they might ostracise offenders who refused to desist, or they might shelter the abused child.[166] The most egregious cases they might report to child protection officers or, as a last resort, to the police. If the law failed, "rough justice" might still be evoked — sometimes leading to further police intervention. By the late Victorian years, however, there was sufficient consensus between popular and official moral codes for the law to be used increasingly to deal with such offences.[167]

Not all forms of family abuse were 'policed' by the popular code. As one clergyman put it: "A beaten wife did not

Anti-Semite. A Psychological Study in a London Borough (London, 1954), p. 63; H. McCleod, *Class and Religion in the Late Victorian City* (London, 1974), note 10, p. 120; See also C. Chinn, *They worked all their lives. Women of the urban poor in England, 1880-1939* (Manchester, 1988), pp. 41-43; E. Roberts, *A Woman's Place. An Oral History of Working-Class Women 1890-1940* (Oxford, 1984), p. 192; Hood and Joyce, "Three Generations", p. 146. And cf. P. Hall, *London Voices, London Lives* (Bristol, 2007), p. 54

[165] G. O'Neill, *My East End. Memories of Life in Cockney London* (London, 1999), pp. 84, 87. See also Hood and Joyce, "Three Generations", p. 147.

[166] A. Davin, *Growing Up Poor. Home, School and Street in London 1870-1914* (London, 1996), p. 37.

[167] L.A. Jackson, *Child sexual abuse in Victorian England* (London, 2000), p. 40; idem., "Law, Order and Violence", in A. Werner (ed.), *Jack the Ripper and the East End* (London, 2008), p. 132.

matter ..." Inspector Pearn of Bethnal Green said a man might beat his wife to death, but a good funeral would bring absolution from the women of the neighbourhood "who say, as Pearn has heard them say 'But he can't be so bad poor man, look what a handsome burial he gave her.'" As Anna Martin claimed, not one wife beating case in one hundred was reported to the police, which should give pause to those who argue that violent crime declined during these years.[168] Anyway, the police tended to follow the popular code in these cases. They were always reluctant to interfere in domestic rows, unless they spilled into the street, since they knew that wives were almost invariably reluctant to give evidence against violent husbands, and quarreling partners could turn their ire on the constable. A policeman who witnessed the murder of a wife by her husband in Bow Road in 1879 failed to interfere "'because I thought they were man and wife.'"[169] Violence between a man and woman unrelated by marriage, however, could inspire intervention, with groups sometimes holding the assailant until the constable arrived.[170]

There were other forms of violence that were left to the popular code to deal with. As with cases of domestic violence, male combatants could resent the presence of the policeman and turn upon him. Male-on-male violence was typically disregarded and unreported, for reasons bound up with notions of masculinity. As were, it seems, conflicts between young factory girls in box, brush, rope, jam and match factories. Booth reported that these girls had "great liberty, being financially independent, and practically uncontrolled by their parents." Duckworth was told of the girls in Bryant and May's match factory in Bow, which employed some 2,000 girls when busy: "Rough & rowdy but not bad morally. They fight with their fists to settle their differences, not in the factory for that is forbidden, but in the streets when

---

[168] Police Walks, B 350, f. 19; E. Ross, "'Fierce Questions and Taunts': Married Life in Working-Class London, 1870-1914", *Feminist Studies*, vol. 8 (1982), p. 591.

[169] Cited in E. Ross, ibid, p. 592.

[170] N. Tomes, "A 'Torrent of Abuse': Crimes of Violence Between Working-Class Men and Women in London, 1840-1875", *Journal of Social History*, (1978), p. 337.

they leave work in the evening. A ring is formed, they fight like men and are not interfered with by the Police." Towards such customary forms of resolving disputes, the police obviously turned a blind eye.[171]

Factory girls standing outside a hot joint shop or eating house, c. 1900

It is clear from this evidence that working-class Londoners by the 1890s were willing to bring, and capable of

[171] Gamon, *The London Police Court*, p. 14; S. D'Cruze, "'Men behaving badly?': masculinity and the uses of violence, 1850-1900", in idem. (ed.), *Everyday Violence in Britain, 1850-1950. Gender and Class* (Harlow, 2000), p. 42; Police Walks, B 346, ff. 75, 77 (Carter). See Clara Collet, "Women's Work", in Booth, *Life and Labour*, Poverty, vol. 4, pp. 322, 325. Police court magistrate, Montagu Williams, was also of the view that the police were good to the match girls and "a constable will rarely interfere with them unless positively compelled to do so": *Round London*, p. 16.

bringing, some level of discipline to bear on their streets, whether to deter illegal activity or to manage numerous instances of anti-social behaviour, all without the recorded intervention of the police. On occasion, they were also willing to call upon police assistance, either because they accepted that the police had a right to intervene, or because the social order, ordinarily maintained by the rules of everyday interactions, had been breached or threatened. In 1888, Henry Webb, a disabled boy from Stepney, was carrying laundry for mangling through Tenter Buildings, when his grandmother relieved him of the bundle and told him to wait. She never came back, so he got in touch with the police.[172] Cooperation with the police was enlarging, though doubtless for some time yet was contingent, selective, and strategic.

In the police's relationship with the metropolitan poor, we should not underestimate their social welfare role. The police may have been reluctant to intervene in domestic disputes, but they did not always ignore them. A woodcarver of Hackney was charged in June 1898 with assaulting his wife. The constable said he had heard screams coming from the house and knocked for admission. He found a woman lying on the floor in pain, who said she would charge her husband with assault. In the same month, a night porter of a casual ward was charged with assaulting his wife. At 11 p.m. on a Friday night, a constable heard children screaming "Murder." He went into the prisoner's house and saw him beating the woman with great violence. The constable, who took the prisoner into custody, treated him "very roughly, calling him 'a cowardly humbug' for striking a woman." The police were also commonly called upon to arbitrate disputes between husbands and wives, neighbours and friends, parents and children. Anna Martin cited the case of Mrs. H, whose husband had thrown her and the four children out of the house when she asked for rent money. The policeman who found her walking the streets at two in the morning went back with her to see if the husband was asleep and it was safe to go back in. When children got lost,

---

[172] Cited in W.J. Fishman, *East End 1888* (Nottingham, 2008; first pub., 2005), p. 229.

parents would ask the police for help. As a child, Arthur Harding was lost and found by the police, taken to Kingsland Road police station, given a slice of bread and jam, and walked home. Around 1895, aged nine, having slept rough for three weeks, Harding was found by the police in an empty house and taken to Stepney Causeway to Dr. Barnardo's. The police also turned a blind eye to some children's activities, allowing them to bathe naked in the Regent's Canal, to pile up wood from Spitalfields market on an old burial ground for bonfire night.[173]

The police were there also to offer support at moments of tragedy caused by fire, illness, accident, or suicide. It was the police the public would turn to when a serious accident occurred in the home, since medical help cost money and was hard to procure. A policeman roused Jasper's parents at eleven at night to tell them that their daughter, who was in hospital, "was dangerously ill and wasn't expected to live." A policeman was stationed at the Bridge of Sighs, which separated the east and west basins of the London Docks in Wapping, from 3pm to 7am to prevent people from attempting suicide. Attempted suicide, inside as well as outside the home, increasingly ended in arrest due to an increasing readiness to fetch the nearest policeman. Indeed, over half of all cases of attempted suicide reported in England and Wales in 1872-3 came from the metropolitan police. At the worst of times, moreover, the police were not averse to providing direct relief. The Hoxton market district in Shoreditch was a warm shop for the police; no policeman dared walk down it alone. "The feelings of this neighbourhood were much touched in the hard winter of 1895", said Duckworth, "when the police opened a subscription among themselves & themselves distributed the bread & soup tickets to the poor whether notorious characters or not."[174]

---

[173] *Hackney Gazette*, 15 June 1898; *Lloyd's Weekly Newspaper*, 12 June 1898; A. Martin, "The Mother and Social Reform", *The Nineteenth Century*, vol. 73 (1913), p. 1066; Samuel, *East End Underworld*, pp. 34-38, 62. Police Walks, B 348, f. 115 (Inspector Mason, Islington Division): "When there is a domestic row the police don't interfere. But if it comes out of doors they have to."

[174] A.S. Jasper, *A Hoxton Childhood* (London, 1971), p. 91; Police Walks, B

Neighbourhoods still existed, of course, where the popular code was not alone a competing or alternative norm of law and order, but an aggressively countervailing norm. The police, aware of their limitations, commonly left such areas to supervise themselves, interfering only when absolutely necessary, and only when crime spilled beyond designated boundaries. These areas were largely self-policing, which is another way of saying that a good deal of illegal activity was tolerated and hidden from police sight. In such districts as the Nichol in Bethnal Green, the wage-based economy was supplemented by a hidden or black economy of scavenging, barter and petty theft. As Henrietta Barnett argued: "There is no strong line of demarcation between the casual labourer, the unskilled worker, and those who from time to time do some sharp practice, or 'help themselves to a bit' without asking." Arthur Harding's memoir is an important text for understanding this late Victorian political economy of crime, in which thieving and the buying and selling of stolen goods was a daily social convention more than a form of deviance. Harding's crippled mother, making daily eight gross of matchboxes for 1s. 8d, was willing to accept any supplement to the family budget, however obtained. Charles Booth wrote of boys who saw nothing wrong in stealing; "they are only ashamed of being caught; and in this course of conduct they are often borne out by their parents. 'If one of them brings home a hock of bacon, his mother cooks it and asks no questions.'" In these areas, too, shopkeepers were willing to go along with popular sentiment. If a policeman caught a boy taking coal from outside a shop, said Arthur Harding, "[the shopkeeper] wouldn't charge him, he'd say 'I'd sooner lose the bag of coal than cause trouble.'" Finally, other forms of illegal activity — drinking, gambling, fighting, theft, and receiving — were kept from the prying eyes of the police. And defiance of the School Board was a form of heroism against the

---

350, f. 223 (Drew); B 352, f. 15 (Barker); O. Anderson, *Suicide in Victorian and Edwardian England* (Oxford, 1987), p. 287; ibid., B 352, f. 177 (Ryeland). See also B. Weinberger and H. Reinke, "A Diminishing Functon? A Comparative Historical Account of Policing in the City", *Policing and Society*, vol. 1 (1991), pp. 214-15.

forces of law and order.[175]

It was in these areas where the police were regarded with the greatest suspicion, and where they could be challenged for control of the streets, not only by costermongers and not only over street and Sunday trading. It was axiomatic that the police were the enemy and to be avoided. A refrain that Louis Heren grew up with in Shadwell, an area of Irish Catholics and Polish Jews, expresses this antipathy: "If you know a good copper, kill him before he goes bad." Walter Southgate's neighbour, Mrs. May, controlled drunken revelers singing outside her house on Saturday night by emptying the chamber pot over them. "She'd have called in the police", said Southgate, "but that would have been against the strict code." Many refused to 'come copper', or give evidence in a criminal case, even when they were the victim. The police 'gaze' was inverted in these districts: 'rooks' or 'crows' guarded places where illegal gambling occurred. Women helped thwart the police by giving asylum to young thieves or providing a means of escape. Crowds often challenged officers arresting people and occasionally succeeded in effecting a rescue. And little quarter was given to the 'copper's nark' who gave information to the police.[176]

---

[175] Wise, *The Blackest Streets*, p. 104; Hobbs, *Doing the Business*, p. 156; S. Henry, *The Hidden Economy. The Context and Control of Borderline Crime* (London, 1978), pp. 5, 12-13; J. Marriott, *The Culture of Labourism. The East End Between the Wars* (Edinburgh, 1991), p, 172 (for costermongers and the police); H.O. Barnett, "East London and Crime", *National Review*, No. 70 (1888), p. 437; Samuel, *East End Underworld*, p. 44; Booth, *Life and Labour*, Final Volume, p. 139. See also S. Humphries, "Steal to Survive: The Social Crime of Working Class Children, 1890-1940", *Oral History Journal*, vol. 9 (1981), pp. 30-32; C. Chinn, *They worked all their lives*, pp. 70-1; E. Ross, *Love and Toil*, p. 151.

[176] L. Heren, *Growing Up Poor in London* (London, 1973), p. 79; Southgate, *That's the Way it Was*, p. 81-2; Leeson, *Lost London*, p. 62; A. Croll, "Street disorder, surveillance and shame: regulating behaviour in the public spaces of the late Victorian British town", *Social History*, vol. 24 (1999), p. 265; Paget, "The London Police Courts", p. 388. Walter Southgate insisted that people "settled their disputes and differences without resort to law." He continued: "They had a great respect for the police but shut up like clams whenever the law began to pry. ... In the presence of strangers and the police the cockney knew nothing, saw nothing and heard nothing ... " We

By the end of the nineteenth century, however, overt resistance to the police was largely confined to socially marginalized groups, living in areas that were in the minority even in the East End. One of the important findings of Booth's study was that the *lumpenproletariat* or residuum of criminal and casual poor (classes A and B) amounted to only 13 per cent of the East End population. Nor was the East End a morass of poor and criminal streets; the poorest class of street constituted only 1.5 per cent of all streets. In 1889, a dozen patches of black appeared on the poverty map, grouped around a few notorious streets: Old Nichol Street and Mount Street in Shoreditch; Great Pearl Street, Flower and Dean Street, Thrawl Street, and Dorset Street in Whitechapel. By the time of the 1898 survey, these areas were less prominent still, and starting to improve.[177]

At the time of the Ripper killings in September 1888, the Rev. Samuel Barnett, founder of Toynbee Hall in Commercial Street, reminded readers of *The Times* that: "The greater part of Whitechapel is as orderly as any part of London and the life of most of its inhabitants is more moral than that of many whose vices are hidden by greater wealth." A member of a vigilante body formed by Toynbee Hall residents to patrol the Whitechapel streets between 11 p.m. and 3 a.m. was struck by the lack of rowdyism and robbery. "No Toynbee man was ever molested, and I have always been completely skeptical of the stories of places in London which were not safe to enter at night." Henrietta Barnett, wife of Samuel, also complained at the way

---

hear an echo of this sentiment in Booth's remark that London provides "the maximum freedom of conduct": "Even criminals find it their best hiding-place. To ask no questions is commonly regarded as the highest form of neighbourliness": Booth, *Life and Labour*, Religious Influences, p. 429, cited in B. Harrison, "The Public and Private in Modern Britain", in P. Burke, et al (eds.), *Civil Histories: Essays Presented to Sir Keith Thomas* (Oxford, 2000), p. 348. It was in such areas, finally, that leadership was typically assumed by publicans, bookies, and the like.

[177] L. Vaughan, D.C. Clark, and O. Sahbaz, "Space and exclusion: the relationship between physical segregation, economic marginalization and poverty in the city", Paper presented to Fifth International Space Syntax Symposium, Deft, Holland, UCL Eprints, p. 3.

East Enders were depicted as "degraded and crime-stained." The bulk of inhabitants, she said, were law-abiding, "with consciences which they keep alive, and a moral code which, if low, is nevertheless obeyed."[178]

The police generally concurred. Superintendent Arnold of H Division informed Chief Commissioner James Monro that "brawling and fighting" occurred among "the low class of persons to be found in Whitechapel, but not nearly to such an extent as might be expected and is generally believed by persons not resident in the district." The superintendent of J Division, Bethnal Green, compiled the arrests made in the year to July 1890 in the Boundary Street area, better known as the Nichol. Of the 214 arrests in a population of 5,700, a third were for being drunk and disorderly, a sixth were for assaults on the police, a sixth for gambling, and one fifth for stealing, unlawful possession, pickpocketing, domestic violence, and assaults on women combined. The serious crimes of stabbing, wounding, indecent assault, and burglary together accounted for only six arrests in the year. As for murder, there was but one in the Nichol between 1885 and 1895, a case of a shoemaker and heavy drinker killing his common-law wife — confirming the fact, with due deference to Jack the Ripper, that women were most at risk of being murdered by kin in their home. Far from being a police no-go area, finally, a handful of policemen chose to live in the Nichol. If further refutation of the exaggerated descriptions of these areas were needed, it came in July 1901 when a *Daily Mail* report, entitled "The Worst Street in London", claiming that in Dorset Street, Spitalfields, the lodging houses were "the head centres of the shifting criminal population of London", and the police had to patrol in pairs, was indignantly rebutted by the inhabitants of the street.[179]

---

[178] Barnett cited in Marriott, *Beyond the Tower*, p. 172 (*Times*, 19 Sept. 1888); Wise, *The Blackest Streets*, pp. 105-6; H.O. Barnett, "East London and Crime", p. 433.

[179] Evans and Skinner, *The Ultimate Jack the Ripper Companion*, pp. 470-71; Wise, *The Blackest Streets*, pp. 99-100; P. Chassaigne, "Londres 1900: assassins, crimes et process", *L'Histoire*, vol. 154 (1992), p. 34; idem., "Le Crime de Sang a Londres a L'Epoque Victorienne: Essai D'Interpretation

Even in these areas, honor among thieves was not assured. Arthur Harding was sent to juvenile reformatory in 1903 for stealing a watch and chain from a young printer who was playing pitch-and-toss in Brick Lane. The printer knew Harding and his mate by name. "Well, he done a thing I never thought he would do", wrote Harding, "he went to the police and Peaky and I were arrested." Nor were all criminals created equal. Harding had nothing but contempt for those involved in the white slave traffic or brothel keeping. And criminal families seem to have tried to steer children away from thieving. Even in these areas, finally, mundane responsibilities bulked large. Harding confirmed that the first and last duty of all residents in the Nichol was to pay the rent, since it was so hard to find a new abode.[180]

In most places the issue was less the criminal reputation of the "ghetto" in question, than what Judith Walkowitz called the "tense and fragile social ecology between rough and respectable elements."[181] The divide in the working classes between the respectable and the rough was essentially an economic divide, with strong moral overtones. It was the split between regular and casual labour markets; it was the split between those who practiced self-help and organized mutual aid in the cause of an independent life, and those who had a life style of 'immediate gratification', hostage to economic circumstance. Of course, Victorian society was never so easily divisible into taxonomies of "respectable-residuum." As Ellen Ross has argued, people socialized across the rough-respectable divide; ties of neighbourhood, kinship and occupation overrode the boundaries between rough and respectable. Respectability, moreover, could be a repertoire to disarm authority, a meretricious performance

Des Modeles De Violence", *Histoire, economie et societe*, vol. 12 (1993), pp. 516-18; idem., "Jack l'eventreur: l'exception ou la regle", *Histoire, economie et societe*, vol. 8 (1989), pp. 516-18; Marriott, *Beyond the Tower*, 172; *Daily Mail*, 16 July 1901, reprinted in www.casebook.org
[180] Samuel, *East End Underworld*, p. 74; Wise, *The Blackest Streets*, p. 74; Hood and Joyce, "Three Generations", p. 144.
[181] J.R. Walkowitz, "Jack the Ripper", p. 566.

for the benefit of rent collector or charity agent.[182]

A socialist orator talking to the unemployed, c. 1900

Yet the distinction has merit. As Marc Brodie argued, we should take Charles Booth's more sanguine view of East End poverty at face value: that almost everywhere comfort predominated over poverty. If 38 per cent of the East End population was said to be in poverty (classes A though D), 62 per cent was in comfort, the bulk of whom were better-off workers and artisans earning regular wages. Along the same lines, historians have dwelt too much upon the casual labour force, drawn from the ranks of the unskilled and semi-skilled, and employed largely in transport and building. Brodie has challenged this image of overwhelming casualization. Of the 180-190,000

[182] J. McCalman, "Respectability and Working-Class Politics in Late-Victorian London", *Historical Studies*, vol. 19 (1980), 112; B. Martin, *A Sociology of Contemporary Cultural Change* (Oxford, 1981), pp. 61-2, 71; Ross, *Love and Toil*, p. 12; note 2, p. 229; T.R.C. Brydon, "Poor, Unskilled and Unemployed: Perceptions of the English Underclass, 1889-1914", M.A. thesis, 2001, McGill University, p. 110.

adult working men in the East End, 55,000 were in unskilled jobs, of whom two-thirds were in receipt of regular wages; only 18-19,000 were casually or irregularly employed manual workers, or approximately 10 per cent of all employed males.[183]

Booth's police guides were convinced that streets had their 'rough' and 'respectable' ends, distinguished by the outward appearance of houses, the order in the street, and the behaviour of inhabitants. Any uplift in family living standards would motivate a move to better accommodation in the same or a nearby street. In other districts, roughs and respectables lived segregated lives, the latter steering clear of the rough streets. If the boundaries between 'rough' and 'respectable' were never hard and fast, the enlarging influence of working-class respectability from 1870 onwards, reinforced by a private, home-centered life style, buttressed by a self-governing associational culture in friendly societies and clubs, led to a more aggressive enforcement of strict standards of behaviour and growing constraints upon those who violated, by conduct, language, or childrearing, the communal mores, and upon children.[184] Indeed, it seems clear

[183] Brodie, *Politics of the Poor*, p. 25; idem., "Artisans and Dossers: The 1886 West End Riots and the East End Casual Poor", *London Journal*, vol. 24 (1999), pp. 40-42; G. Stedman Jones, *Outcast London* (London, 1984), pp. 55, 64-5.

[184] P. Johnson, "Conspicuous Consumption and Working-Class Culture in Late-Victorian and Edwardian Britain", *Transactions of the Royal Historical Society*, 5th ser., vol. 38 (1988), p. 34; Hood and Joyce, "Three Generations", p. 143; M.J. Daunton, "Public Place and Private Space. The Victorian City and the Working-Class Household", in D. Fraser and A. Sutcliffe (eds.), *The Pursuit of Urban History* (London, 1983), pp. 223-4; J. Carter Wood, *Violence and crime in nineteenth-century England* (London, 2004), p. 142; G. Stedman Jones, "The 'cockney' and the nation, 1780-1988", in D. Feldman and G. Stedman Jones (eds.), *Metropolis-London* (London, 1989), p. 309; Booth, *Life and Labour*, Poverty, vol. 1, p. 110 (Table XVIII, Friendly Societies); Harris, *Private Lives*, p. 193; Ross, "Respectability", p. 39; Davin, *Growing Up Poor*, p. 216. Sarah Williams reminds us that Booth claimed the habits of the home were stronger than the precepts of school and church: "The Problem of Belief: The Place of Oral History in the Study of Popular Religion", *Oral History*, vol. 24 (1996), p. 27. In 1889, there were approximately 47,000 Friendly Society members in East London, the highest numbers in Shoreditch, Poplar, and Whitechapel. The Societies provided

that workers themselves played an important part in the process of demarcation between the working and criminal classes.[185]

The respectable working class welcomed the greater order and safety of the streets, the greater security of property and person. New standards of respectability included the notion that violence against women was 'unmanly', and that male-on-male violence in street or pub was excessive.[186] Booth's police guides and clerical informants were certainly of the view that the East End was a much less rough place than previously. P.C. Ryeland of the Hoxton subdivision said his district had deteriorated — "the poor were as poor & a rough class had come in. But the roughness today was not to be compared with the roughness of 10 or 15 years ago. He can find no reason for the change." Superintendent Weston insisted that roughness was decreasing, "not rapidly but he thought surely even in Bethnal Green." Inspector Webb, from the same sub-division, told Duckworth in the vernacular: "'But roughness aint nothing now anywhere in London to what it was when I first joint.'" Even the Irish cockneys came in for the occasional plaudit. The inhabitants of Pennington Street in St. Georges-in-the-East caused trouble to the police from occasional quarrels, but, said Inspector Reid, "'for months they are quiet & since dock labour has been more regular the tone & behaviour of the people is quieter than it used to be.'" Booth's report on St. George's and Whitechapel claimed that there had been "an especially marked change for the better in the behaviour and habits of the lowest social stratum. Such scenes of unmitigated savagery as old inhabitants have witnessed are

---

sickness and death benefits. There were also forms of club life operating under the aegis of churches, missions and university settlement houses.

[185] Ignatieff, "State, Civil Society", p. 91; B. Weinberger, "The Criminal Class and the Ecology of Crime", *Historical Social Research*, vol. 15 (1990), p. 137.

[186] D. Taylor, "Policing and Community", in K. Laybourn (ed.), *Social conditions, Status and Community 1860-c.1920* (Thrupp, 1997), p. 120. The popular desire for urban order is evident, too, in the thousands of complaints of unsanitary conditions submitted to the London County Council: S. Pennybacker, *A Vision for London 1889-1914* (London, 1995), pp. 200-01.

unknown now."[187]

Crime, too, was thought to have decreased. "Crime", said detective inspector Morgan from King's Cross Road, "had been decreasing all over London in the last ten years especially crime with violence." "As a whole", said Superintendent Vedy, "crime was decreasing especially crime with violence. People are less brutal than they used to be." Mr. Neil of St. Matthias, just north of Poplar High Street, said his was not a criminal district. Mr. Galt of the London City Missionary, north of the East India Dock Road, where most men had irregular work in connection with shipping, and where drinking and gambling were prevalent, reported: "very little crime; people are working class and law abiding. At the time of the great frost [in 1895] when nearly all were out of work, there was not a single arrest for theft altho' thousands of pounds worth of goods were exposed in Chrisp Street [Poplar's largest street market]." Booth concluded: "... in spite of outbursts of 'Hooliganism', there is much less street violence; and such scenes of open depravity as occurred in years gone by do not happen now."[188]

Respectability was above all self-discipline. Hence, an endnote to this section on community self-regulation is what John Carter Wood has described, following Norbert Elias, as the transformation of external structures of control into internal

---

[187] Police Walks, B 352, f. 133 (Ryeland); B 350, f. 41 (Weston); B 352, f. 15 (Webb); B 351, f. 29 (Reid); Booth, *Life and Labour*, Religious Influences, vol. 2, p. 5.

[188] Police Walks, B 353, f. 215 (Morgan); B 349, f. 31 (Vedy); B 170, f. 55 (Neil); B 172, f. 14 (Galt); Booth, *Life and Labour*, Final Volume, p. 201. Rev. Canon Barnett, Warden of Toynbee Hall, also considered that the condition of the East End was better, "measured by moral standards": *Royal Commission on Alien Immigration*, Evidence PP. 1903 [Cd. 1742], vol. IX, q. 17554. See also R. McKibbin, "Class and Poverty in Edwardian England", in idem, *Ideologies of Class*, p. 182. "Hooliganism" hit the headlines in the summer of 1898, inspiring Clarence Rook's *Daily Chronicle* articles, which appeared later as *Hooligan Nights* (1899). The "moral panic" around the hooligan expressed the concern for the disciplinary hiatus between school and work. See B. Schwarz, "Night Battles: Hooligan and Citizen", in M. Nava and A. O'Shea (eds.), *Modern Times. Reflections on a century of English modernity* (London, 1996), 106.

inhibitions. As he concluded: "Community self-policing, by and large, gave way to the policing of the self." The point is that of socialization: a long-term growth of self-control in daily life, of strengthening personal control of feelings and impulses, becoming ever more deeply ingrained in personality and conscience. Grace Foakes' father pilfered tea one day from the docks, and was sacked on the spot for stealing, having been stopped and searched by a dock policeman. "In a community such as ours", said Foakes, "this was indeed a disgrace and it was many days before my mother could bring herself to go out. I think she felt worse than anyone about it." Mr. Dodd of the Shaftesbury Memorial Mission, Poplar, who lived among the working class, said there was more thrift among them than ten years ago, concluding: "A spirit of self-respect is taking hold of them."[189]

Chrisp Street Market, looking south, early 20th century

---

[189] J. Carter Wood, *Violence and crime*, pp. 140-1; G. Foakes, *Between High Walls* (London, 1972); Police Walks, B 172, f. 39 (Dodd). See also Martin, *Contemporary Cultural Change*, p. 74; F.M.L. Thompson, "Social Control in Victorian Britain", *Economic History Review*, vol. XXXIV (1981), pp. 190, 195-6; D. Garland, *Punishment and Modern Society* (Chicago, 1990), pp. 288-89.

X

Thus far, little has been said about the self-regulation of ethnic communities in the East End. Booth's police informants were well aware of their existence. The riverside district of Pennyfields and Limehouse Causeway was home to the opium dens of Lascars, Indians, Japanese, and Chinese. The Secretary's report on this district in the Booth survey stated: "As far as one can see it is a very harmless vice for Asiatics & their existence is winked at by the police." Inspector Carter thought they were no threat: "The Japs and Chinamen are as a rule quiet & easy to deal with. ... The Chinaman has a great respect for authority."[190] The Irish quarters, as we have seen, were a different kettle of fish. The only men capable of restraining the Limehouse and Poplar Irish were, according to the police themselves, the priests. Priests went from house to house, "and as they enter the fighting stops. They even do not hesitate to lay their own hands on an offender in order to drag him to justice if the occasion demands it. They enter freely & alone where the police could only go safely in a posse." The residents of Sophia and Rook Streets, south of Fenian Barracks, resisted police authority, respecting only the priesthood. On the other side of the East India Dock Road was Father Lawless' Catholic Church. "'He is a wonderful man, he can stop a row where we police are of no use at all'," said Carter; "'Once Father Lawless is there the people seem to be ashamed & they slip away one by one & gradually all is quiet: they do not even start it again as soon as his back is turned.'"[191]

---

[190] Booth Collection, Notebooks on the Religious Influences Series, A 33(i), f. 49; Police Walks, B 346, ff. 101, 119-129 (Carter). See also J. Seed, "Limehouse Blues: Looking for Chinatown in the London Docks, 1900-40", *History Workshop Journal*, Issue 62 (2006), pp. 59, 67.

[191] Booth Collection, Notebooks on Religious Influences Series, A 32 (i), ff. 29-30; Police Walks, B 346, f. 97 (Carter); B 180, f. 67 (Father Lawless). For the German inhabitants of the East End, working largely in sugar-baking and sugar–refining, see H. Llewellyn Smith, "Influx of Population (East London)", in Booth, *Life and Labour*, Poverty, vol. 3, p. 102; P. Panayi, "The German Poor and Working classes in Victorian and Edwardian London", in G. Alderman and C. Holmes (eds.), *Outsiders and Outcasts: Essays in Honour of William J. Fishman* (London, 1993), pp. 55, 60; Gilda

There is one ethnic community that is particularly worth dwelling upon: the Jewish East End. The influx of Russian Jews began in 1881-2, in the wake of the pogroms of those years. The years of highest immigration of Russian and Polish Jews were 1891-2, 1899-1901, and 1903-6 (as Russian Jews fled to escape military service in the Russo-Japanese war). According to immigration statistics, over one-fifth of Jewish immigrants who landed were penniless, and a further 15 per cent had less than 10 shillings per head. Entire families tended to migrate, resulting in a high proportion of women, young adults and children among the Jewish migrants. In 1901, almost 70,000 of the 120,000 East End Jews were under 20 years of age. By 1905, the Jewish population in London, immigrant and native-born, was over 140,000 of which some 120,000 lived in the borough of Stepney. Jews made up 40 per cent or more of the population of Whitechapel and St. George's. Social investigators described what Russell and Lewis called "an alien community", an enclosed and defensible space, peculiar in mother tongue, religious rituals and rules, and cultural habits, and sustained by sweated trades.[192] George Duckworth's description encapsulated his Whitechapel experience as follows:

> Great mess in Jewish streets — fishes heads, paper of
> all colours, bread ... orange peel in abundance. The

O'Neill, *My East End. Memories of Life in Cockney London* (London, 2000), p. 51.

[192] See Feldman, *Englishmen and Jews* (New Haven, 1994), pp. 148, 157-59, 170-72; idem., "The importance of being English. Jewish immigration and the decay of liberal England", in Feldman and Jones, *Metropolis-London*, p. 56; Marks, *Model Mothers. Jewish Mothers and Maternity Provision in East London, 1870-1939* (Oxford,1994), pp. 11, 14, 18-19; Lipman, "Jewish settlement in the East End-1840-1940", in Newman, *The Jewish East End*, pp. 34, 40; J. White, *London in the Nineteenth Century* (London, 2007), p. 154; C. Russell and H.S. Lewis, *The Jew in London. A Study of Racial Character and Present-Day Conditions* (New York, 1901), pp. 7, 9, 12. Lewis lived for many years in Toynbee Hall. See also L.P. Gartner, *The Jewish Immigrant in England, 1870-1914* (Detroit, 1960), pp. 16-17; *Report of the Royal Commission on Alien Immigration*, PP. 1903 [Cd. 1741-1], vol. IX, Appendix, Table XXXV, c.

constant whirr of the sewing machine or tap of the Hammer as you pass through the streets: women with dark abundant hair, olive complexions, no hats but shawls — Children well-fed & dressed. Dark beards, fur caps & long boots of men — The feeling of being in a foreign Town.[193]

The Jewish East End was a circle of two square miles, bounded on the west or City side by the Minories, Houndsgate and Bishopsgate, on the north by Buxton Street and the Great Eastern Railway, on the east by the London hospital, and on the south by Cable Street. Jews overwhelmingly occupied the streets within this circle. It was the area that Jack the Ripper made infamous. Within this area, there were four distinct Jewish districts (colored blue on George Arkell's map, which accompanied Russell and Lewis's *The Jew in London*). The first district lay between Commercial Street, Whitechapel High Street, and Houndsditch. This included Wentworth Street, "thronged every day by stalls, both buyers & sellers nearly but not altogether Jews", according to Duckworth, "women bareheaded, bewigged, coarse woolen shawls over shoulders, more like a foreign market scene than anything English." A provisioning ground for the Wentworth Street stalls was Cox's Square, "rough Jews, cellars used for fruit, cases of oranges, lemons, stacked in the square."[194]

---

[193] Police Walks, B 351, f. 47 (Reid). Reflecting on the changes that had taken place in the past fifteen years in Whitechapel and St. George's-in-the-East, Charles Booth was most impressed by "the increase of the Jewish population. It has been like the slow rising of a flood. Street after street is occupied. Family follows family… each small street or group of houses invaded tends to become entirely Jewish": Booth, *Life and Labour*, Religious Influences, vol. 2, p. 1. See also J. Bronstein, "Rethinking the 'Readmission': Anglo-Jewish History and the Immigration Crisis", in G.K. Behlmer and F. Leventhal (eds.), *Singular Continuities: Tradition, Nostalgia, and Identity in Modern British Culture* (Stanford, 2000), p. 39.

[194] Russell and Lewis, *The Jew in London*, Notes on Map, pp. xxxiv-xlv, and p. 13; Police Walks, B 351, ff. 109, 111 (French). See R. Kalman, "The Jewish East End — Where Was It?", in Newman, *The Jewish East End*, p. 14; *Report of the Royal Commission on Alien Immigration*, Evidence, PP. 1903 [Cd. 1742], vol. IX, q. 6576 (John Foot, Chief Sanitary Inspector for Bethnal Green).

Jewish East London

The second district was further south between Great Alie and Great Prescott Streets; the third further east in St. George's between Cannon Street Road and Backchurch Lane. The final district was the large triangle formed by Commercial Street, Old Montague Street and Hanbury Street. According to Duckworth, "a greater mixture of well to do, poor & very poor in adjacent houses or even in the same house, among Jews than among Gentiles." In this last district, the red patches (where non-Jews predominated) represented lodging houses, while in the third district in St. George's the red patches represented Irish carmen and dockers "who have no dealings with the Jews and will not live with them."[195] Nor were Jews admitted as tenants in dwellings erected by the breweries and the Great Eastern Railway Company. Yet the Jewish area continued to expand.

Jews moved eastwards along Whitechapel Road and Commercial Road and into the streets between these highways. Further east still, past Stepney Green in Beaumont Square: "Great influx of Jews here who are gradually driving out the Gentiles", according to Inspector Drew. And around Eastfield Street (in the Carr Street area), Jews were beginning to buy up property; they

---

[195] Police Walks, B 351, f. 155 (French).

"'dare not put in any Jewish tenants just yet, they wd have too hot a time'," said Drew, "' they will wait till they have got a whole street, then Jewish tenants will come in en bloc, rents will be raised & the former owners given notice to quit.'"[196] Further north in Bethnal Green, between 1890 and 1902, Jews moved into Bacon, Hare, and Fuller Streets, and also to the other side of Bethnal Green Road in Church, Chambord and Gossett Streets. In all these streets, the original inhabitants were ousted.

The Jewish districts were renowned for their high rents, sub-letting, and overcrowding. Spitalfields had the largest proportion of overcrowding in East London. Nearly half the inhabitants of Whitechapel lived in one-room dwellings, with three occupants per room, on average; rents went up over 80 per cent between 1890 and 1903. The frugality and temperance of the Jewish workman, it was said, allowed him to devote a higher proportion of his earnings to rent than the native worker. The congestion of the Jewish population was aggravated by industrial conditions. In the typically Jewish trades of tailoring, boot- and shoe-making, and furniture, workers were employed in small workshops, or did outwork in their own homes. These trades were renowned for sweated labour conditions, and were subject to seasonal fluctuations. Whether waiting for work in the slack season or working long hours in the busy season, it was a great convenience to live in the immediate vicinity of work and close to the business district in the City of London.[197]

[196] Police Walks, B 350, ff. 55, 151 (Drew).
[197] Feldman, "The importance of being English", p. 60; Marks, *Model Mothers*, p. 62; I.A. Hourwich, "The Jewish Laborer in London", *Journal of Political Economy*, vol. 13 (1904), p. 96. For Jewish trades, see Beatrice Potter, "The Tailoring Trade", in Booth, *Life and Labour*, Poverty, vol. 4, p. 46; Russell and Lewis, *The Jew in London*, pp. 20, 66-69, 75-82; V.D. Lipman, *A Century of Social Service 1859-1959. The Jewish Board of Guardians* (London, 1959), note 1, p. 119; Feldman, *Englishmen and Jews*, pp. 163, 207, 241; Marks, *Model Mothers*, pp. 20-21; D. Englander, "Booth's Jews", in Englander and O'Day, *Retrieved Riches*, pp. 308-09; P. Johnson, "Economic Development and Industrial Dynamism in Victorian London", *London Journal*, vol. 21 (1996), p. 33; Samuel, *East End Underworld*, p. 127. Russell and Lewis said this of the Jew as workman: industrious, sober, reliable, also "an inveterate individualist, whose ambition is usually for

Middlesex traders and locals in Middlesex Street, 1899

The police were involved from the start in maintaining order in the Jewish ghetto. Constables met the boats loaded with foreign immigrants at the Iron Gate Stairs on the Thames. The most destitute were directed to the Poor Jews' Temporary Shelter in Tenter Street, Whitechapel, or the Jewish Soup Kitchen in Fashion Street, Spitalfields. This police work went on for years, only occasionally with violent overtones. In December, 1904, 300 Russian Jews congregated outside the Fournier Street synagogue,

himself rather than for his class. He desires almost invariably to become ultimately a small master, a dealer or a shopkeeper; to live, in short, on profits rather than on wages." (p. 192). Cf. B. Potter, "The Jewish Community (East London)", in Booth, *Life and Labour*, Poverty, vol. 3, pp. 186-87. As with the Jew as gambler (see below), the Jew as "economic man" was a resistant racial stereotype. There was little effective trade union organization: Feldman, *Englishmen and Jews*, pp. 222-25; J. Green, *A Social History of the Jewish East End in London, 1914-1939* (Lewiston, 1991), p. 59; A.J. Kershen, *Uniting the Tailors. Trade Unionism amongst the Tailoring Workers of London and Leeds, 1870-1939* (Ilford, 1995), pp. 135-40.

near Brick Lane, and, said a police report, "threatened to break the doors open if they were not given bread; many are absolutely starving they walk the streets by day and night the shelters being full."[198] The synagogues fed them daily, the police were sent to keep order.

The main threat to public order in the Jewish ghetto was the violence between Jew and non-Jew over housing, jobs, and wages. Conflict was of short duration, however, and restricted to the edges of the foreign quarter where the two races lived in mixed courts or on the same street and where the native population was being driven out.[199] Street battles were designed to define the boundaries of Jewish settlement. Sergeant French told Duckworth that Shepherd Street Buildings had been Jewish but had changed hands and was Gentile again: "The Jews have been turned out by a set of rough English & Irish." In November 1898, Jews trying to move into Ernest Street, Stepney Green, were kept out. In November 1901, Cornwall Street, Shadwell, was the scene of a riot when the dock labourers and carmen were given notice

---

[198] Police Walks, B 351, f.61 (Reid); NA, MEPO 2/ 260, police report 6 Dec. 1904; *Royal Commission on Alien Immigration*, Evidence PP. 1903 [Cd. 1742], vol. IX, q. 7640 (Stephen White, retired CID inspector).

[199] Feldman, "Jews in London, 1880-1914", in R. Samuel (ed.), *Patriotism* (London, 1989), vol. II, p. 212; Russell and Lewis, *The Jew in London*, p. 16; L. Marks, "Jewish women and Jewish prostitution in the East End of London", *Jewish Quarterly*, vol. 34 (1987), p. 7; T. Kushner, "Jew and Non-Jew in the East End of London: Towards an Anthropology of 'Everyday' Relations", in Alderman and Holmes, *Outsiders and Outcasts*, p. 39; A. Lee, "Aspects of the Working-Class Response to the Jews in Britain, 1880-1914", in K. Lunn (ed.), *Hosts, Immigrants and Minorities* (Folkestone, 1980), p. 121; J. White, *Rothschild Buildings*, p.135. As David Englander said: "Police observation … presented the growth of the ghetto not as the natural and irresistible outcome of foreign immigration, but as a negotiated process": Englander, "Jewish East London, 1850-1950", in W.T.R. Pryce, *From Family History to Community History* (Cambridge, 1994), p. 201. Russell and Lewis observed: "Against the Jew as a Jew there seems to be no sort of hostile feeling. … And such hostility as does exist towards the foreign element is neither racial nor religious in character. It is always based either on some special grievance … or — much more rarely — on mere insular objection to all foreign … persons": op. cit., p. 42. Jews would rarely dare to apply for casual work at the docks: Goldman, *East End My Cradle*, p. 142.

to make way, rumor had it, for Jewish residents. In this way, exclusion zones were created, which Jews knew better than to enter. To the east of the Boundary Street clearances in Bethnal Green, between Brick Lane and Chambord Streets, "No Jews have their foot as yet in this district. 'They would not dare to, they wd be so roughly handled'," said Sergeant French.[200] The Old Nicholl in Bethnal Green, before the Boundary Street clearances, was one such exclusion zone. Another was Dorset Street, as was Wapping, between Gravel Lane and Wapping Bridges.

The police were frequently drawn into these intercommunal clashes over housing. Inspector Reid told Duckworth that the Jews in Boyd Street, Whitechapel, could not understand English: "only a trouble to police when ejectments are necessary & neither side can comprehend the other." It was one of the few points of contact, however, between the police and Jews, since the Jewish community was not particularly troublesome. Superintendent Mulvaney claimed that Polish and Russian Jews were "mostly strong socialists." "Their first inclination in coming over here & finding their liberty is to break out but they don't do it long." They were on the whole law abiding. "Not rough towards the police. They knife one another but not those in authority." A few years later, Mulvaney told the Royal Commission on Alien Immigration that few if any of the immigrants were members of "the criminal class."[201]

Probably the most widespread criminal activity among Jews was gambling. The East End was home to numerous gambling clubs or *spielers*, some of which were registered as workmen's clubs. This made it difficult for the police to bring

[200] Police Walks, B 351, ff. 117, 139, 199 (French). See Southgate, *That's the Way it Was*, p. 33; Goldman, *East End My Cradle*, p. 16; Russell and Lewis, *The Jew in London*, p. xliii; Inwood, *City of Cities*, p. 72.
[201] Police Walks, B 351, ff. 69, 71 (Reid); B 350, ff. 43, 45 (Mulvaney). See also *Royal Commission on Alien Immigration*, Evidence PP. 1903 [Cd. 1742], vol. IX, qq. 8358, 8500 (Mulvaney); *Report from the Select Committee on Emigration and Immigration (Foreigners)*, PP. 1889 [311], vol. X, q. 884 (Supt. Thomas Arnold); F. Rocker, *The East End Years. A Stepney Childhood* (London, 1998), p. 56. For clash between Orthodox and Socialist Jews, see *Times*, 20 Sept. 1904, p. 7: "Jewish Riot in the East-End."

scrutiny to bear. Inspector Reid conveyed the withdrawnness of the Jew: "Jews drink very little in the public houses; the police cannot understand them at all. They shut themselves up in their clubs & there is no getting near them."[202] According to Arthur Harding, however, Jewish gambling houses were subject to ritual police raids and arrests (and the associated bribery), the police keeping them open as conduits of information about Jewish anarchists. In June 1897, at the Worship Street police court, 21 foreign Jews living in Whitechapel and Spitalfields were charged with being in a gaming house in Underwood Street, Mile End. The prisoners were ordered to enter into their own recognizances to be of good behaviour for twelve months each in £5. Jews were also involved in illicit distilling. In March 1899, at Thames police court, five Polish Jews, unable to speak English, were charged with manufacturing spirits in an unlicensed house in Mile End and defrauding the inland revenue to a great extent. Heavy fines were handed down.[203]

Jews were also involved in prostitution. In 1887, the Jewish Ladies' Association for Preventive and Rescue Work was told that 20-30 Jewesses thronged about the East India dock gates. The Rev. Arthur Dalton, rector of Stepney Parish, told the Royal Commission on Alien Immigration that around 1890 in Poplar "a large number of our prostitutes were foreigners, and foreign Jewesses." Inspector Drew said there were no prostitutes among the Jewesses in his St. George's-in-the-East subdivision, but Mulvaney claimed there were large numbers of foreign prostitutes in Whitechapel Road and Commercial Road. Data collected from before the First World War in the borough of Stepney showed that 20 per cent of the convictions for brothel-keeping were against Jews (though this figure may reflect a bias against Jews). The "white slave" traffic, finally, was said to be in the hands of Jews, but this was largely a figment of the

---

[202] Police Walks, B 351, f. 87 (Reid). See also *Royal Commission on Alien Immigration*, Evidence PP. 1903 [Cd. 1742], vol. IX, qq. 8487-88 (Mulvaney); O'Day and Englander, *Mr Charles Booth's Inquiry*, p. 77.

[203] Samuel, *East End Underworld*, p. 178; *Reynolds's Newspaper*, 20 June 1897; *Daily News*, 8 March 1899.

anti-alien movement's imagination, a connection the latter exploited nonetheless to secure the passage of the 1905 Aliens Act.[204]

Russell and Lewis showed that most Jewish prisoners were convicted of larceny or receiving stolen property, but concluded that "the proportion of convictions for serious crime amongst the Jews ... is far smaller than amongst the general population." Arthur Harding claimed he learned his criminal apprenticeship among the Jewish pickpockets and receivers of Whitechapel. An increase in juvenile crime in the late 1890s in Whitechapel led to the foundation of a Jewish industrial school, but the number of boys concerned was not large, and Inspector Barker took comfort from the fact that thieving was age-specific: "Very few adult thieves among Jews." Burglary was rare and usually small scale. In August 1899, two Polish Jews were charged with "burglariously entering" a Whitechapel house and attempting to steal clothing worth £5. A detective sergeant caught them in the act. They were committed for trial. In the early twentieth century, the Russian Jewish Bessarabian gang brought a reign of terror to bear upon Jewish shopkeepers, who were reluctant to ask the police for help.[205] Murder was rarer still,

[204] L. Gartner, "Anglo-Jewry and the Jewish International Traffic in Prostitution, 1885-1914", *Association for Jewish Studies Review*, vol. 7-8 (1982-3), p. 150; *Royal Commission on Alien Immigration*, Evidence PP. 1903 [Cd. 1742], vol. IX, q. 10166 (Dalton); Police Walks, B 350, f. 193 (Drew); E.J. Bristow, *Prostitution and Prejudice. The Jewish Fight against White Slavery 1870-1939* (New York, 1983), p. 237; *Royal Commission on Alien Immigration*, Evidence PP. 1903 [Cd. 1742], vol. IX, q. 8469 (Mulvaney); L. Marks, "Jewish women and Jewish prostitution", p. 8; idem., "Race, class and gender: the experience of Jewish prostitutes and other Jewish women in the East End of London at the turn of the century", in J. Grant (ed.), *Women, migration and Empire* (Stoke-on-Trent, 1996), p. 39; B. Gainer, *The Alien Invasion. The Origins of the Aliens Act of 1905* (London, 1972). The Jewish Association for the Protection of Girls and Women strangely accepted the description of prostitution and the international sex trade as a "Jewish crime": P. Knepper, "British Jews and the Racialisation of Crime in the Age of Empire", *British Journal of Criminology*, vol. 47 (2007), p. 75; Bristow, op. cit., pp. 241-42.

[205] Russell and Lewis, *The Jew in London*, pp. 175-6; Kushner, "Jew and

though the rape and murder in June 1887 by Israel Lipski of a co-religionist female living in the same house as him; the anonymous inscription on the wall near one of the Ripper's victims, "The Jews will not be blamed in vain", (which led the police to send reinforcements in September 1888 to Whitechapel to avoid the outbreak of anti-Jewish disturbances); and the fatal stabbing in December 1900 of P.C. Thompson (who had discovered the body of Frances Coles, the last Ripper victim) by an English Jew in Commercial Road — all drew attention to the Jewish East End.[206]

In only three other ways were the police involved with the Jewish community: obstructions by costerrmongers, private quarrels, and anarchists. Jewish costers in the late 1890s tried to make a great street market in Samuel, James, William, and John Streets to the west of the recognized market place in Watney Street, to which the local authorities objected. A couple of hundred were summonsed for obstruction over the next few years, and magistrates inflicted fines, without effect, according to Mulvaney. Second, while Jews were "no physical trouble to the police" and "respecters of authority", according to Inspector Drew, they were a deal of bother: "they bring their private quarrels to the police station each charging the other with crimes;

Non-Jew", p. 40; Police Walks, B 352, ff. 59-63 (Barker); Lloyd's Weekly Newspaper, 13 August 1899; Marriott, Beyond the Tower, p. 296. Jews were under-represented in the prison population: Reports on Volume and Effects of Immigration from E. Europe into United Kingdom, PP 1894 [C. 7406], vol. LXVIII, pp. 60-62, vi: Condition as regards Crime.
206 Chassaigne, "Londres 1900", p. 34 (Lipski); Walkowitz, "Jack the Ripper", pp. 555-56 (for a Jewish shoemaker called "Leather Apron", whom suspicion fixed upon); Inwood, City of Cities, p. 379; D. Englander, "Policing the Ghetto. Jewish East London, 1880-1920", Crime, History & Societies, vol. 14 (2010), p. 43; The Illustrated Police News, 8 Dec. 1900, 29 Dec. 1900; Lloyd's Weekly Newspaper, 16 Dec. 1900; Divall, Scoundrels and Scallywags, p. 104; N. Connell and S.P. Evans, The Man Who Hunted Jack the Ripper. Edmund Reid and the Police Perspective (Cambridge, 1999), p. 91. See also C. Holmes, "East End Crime and the Jewish community", in A. Newman (ed.), The Jewish East End 1840-1939 (Jewish Historical Society of England, 1981). It is sometimes claimed that P.C. Thompson was the only constable who ever saw Jack-the-Ripper, running away after murdering Frances Coles.

it is impossible to believe either."[207] Thirdly, there was a lively if tiny anarchist community of Jewish refugees, with their own newspapers, in the East End. It had emerged in the early 1880s as an integral part of the socialist revival. Anarchists spoke on street corners and at open-air rallies, and were in the beginning preoccupied with organizing industrial protest, which came to a head with the tailors' strike of 1889. Neither via their propaganda nor their trade union activity were they thought to pose a threat to social stability.[208] In the first half of the 1890s, however, a number of explosions and bomb scares, plus the exaggerated media portrayal of foreign Jewish anarchists as violent criminals, brought them to the attention of the Special Branch of the Metropolitan Police, formed in 1883 to suppress Irish terrorism. Special Branch officers would occasionally "shadow" anarchists, attend meetings to take notes of speeches, and raid anarchist clubs and newspaper offices. In general, the police regarded most anarchists as harmless, and ignored the pressure from foreign governments to act against them.[209] It is hard not to agree with Fishman's conclusion that, except for their "militant incursions into strike action", anarchists and their ideas "remained a pernicious irrelevance to immigrant aspirations as a whole."[210]

[207] See S. Pennybacker, "'The millennium by return of post.' Reconsidering London Progressivism, 1889-1907", in Feldman and Jones, *Metropolis-London*, p. 144 and note 61, p. 159; *Royal Commission on Alien Immigration,* Evidence PP. 1903 [Cd. 1742], vol. IX, qq. 8345, 8477-86, 8514; Police Walks, B 350, f. 231 (Drew).

[208] M. Thomas, *Anarchist Ideas and Counter-Cultures in Britain, 1880-1914* (Aldershot, 2005), pp. 13, 49.

[209] B. Porter, *The Origins of the Vigilant State* (London, 1987), pp. 121, 123, 130; H. Shpayer-Makov, "Anarchism in British Public Opinion 1880-1914, *Victorian Studies*, vol. 31 (1988), pp. 487, 495, 515; idem, *The Ascent of the Detective* (Oxford, 2011), p. 133.

[210] W.J. Fishman, *East End Jewish Radicals 1875-1914* (London, 1975), p. 225.

Discovery of the 10th victim: 1891

In all, Jewish crime was rarely violent, subversive, or serious; it was petty, private, and offended mostly against morals. Jewish crime was perplexing more than confrontational. The police never felt at risk in the ghetto, they simply felt at sea. Part of the problem was linguistic. As late as 1903, not a single constable in the entire H or Whitechapel division spoke or understood Yiddish. In December 1904, the Commissioner of Police asked the Home Office to allow a few officers to become conversant with Yiddish, since "the necessity for the police to get more closely in touch with this large population is becoming a serious factor in the police administration." The police were unable to decipher the bills and circulars that were posted, some by members of revolutionary clubs. The metropolitan police never sought to recruit Jews to the force, and Jews were too suspicious of uniformed policemen to want to join.[211]

The police never pretended that the law-abidingness of the Jews owed much to their presence. They were the first to recognize, however, that the arrival of Jews had transformed the character of many rough neighbourhoods. In Whitechapel and Spitalfields, Duckworth reported "betterment" in Hanbury and Church Streets "owing to the incoming of well to do Jews", and in the courts south of Old Montague Street "owing to the displacement of rough English or Irish by poor but quiet Jews." Jews had taken over one end of Great Pearl Street and "'it is probably the Jews who will turn out the prostitutes from the end that is still bad.'" The north side of Flower and Dean Street had made way for the Rothschild Buildings, in which residents were almost exclusively Jewish artisans and their families, and whose lives made a favorable contrast to the lodging houses, prostitutes and criminals at the other end of Flower and Dean Street. In St. George's-in-the-East, two black spots had been removed from Little Turner Street due to "the ousting of the rough and the vicious by foreign Jews" and to the building of Salters Buildings,

---

[211] See D. Englander, "Booth's Jews: The Presentation of Jews and Judaism in Life and Labour of the People in London", *Victorian Studies*, vol. 32 (1989), p. 563, 565; Englander and O'Day, *Retrieved Riches*, pp. 304-07; *Royal Commission on Alien Immigration*, Evidence PP. 1903 [Cd. 1742], vol. IX, qq. 8396-97 (Mulvaney); NA, MEPO 2/ 733; D. Englander, "*Stille Huppah* (Quiet Marriage) Among Jewish Immigrants in Britain", *Jewish Journal of Sociology*, vol. 34 (1992), p. 98; Samuel, *East End Underworld*, p. 78: Harding said of the Jews, "They had bad memories of the police in Russia and weren't fond of giving them information."

tenanted by Jews. In Stepney, what Duckworth termed "probable invasion of Jews" in the Carr Street or Donkey Row area was "'the only prospect the district has of ever becoming better than it is.'" Finally, Inspector Reid of the Leman Street subdivision noted that Jews patronized neither the pawnbroker nor the public house, and some pawnbrokers and publicans in the Jewish quarter were selling up. Booth himself set the seal on all these observations when he wrote, none too delicately, that the Jews acted as "moral scavengers", driving "worse microbes out."[212]

What explains the comparatively low crime rates and law-abidingness of the Jews? Most sources suggest it was a combination of Jewish religion, family structure, temperance, education, and philanthropy, all of which contributed to the greater cohesiveness of the Jewish community. Charles Booth described Judaism as "a family religion, a matter of birth and heritage, even more than belief." His young colleague, Beatrice Potter, in her survey of the Jewish community, described what she called "the moral precepts of Judaism" as "centred in the perfection of family life, in obedience towards parents, in self-devotion for children, in the chastity of the girl, in the support and protection of the wife." She also noted that East End Jews rarely attended the larger synagogues (except on the Day of Atonement), preferring to frequent *chevras*, named after the district in Russia or Poland from which they had emigrated: "self-creating, self-supporting, and self-governing communities", combining the functions of a benefit club with that of public worship and Talmudic study. Secular benefit societies also recruited thousands of East London Jews.[213]

Ernest Aves, one of Booth's investigators, and longtime resident of Toynbee Hall, thought Jews "are often given a clearer

---

[212] Police Walks, B 351, f. 137 (French); B 350, ff. 155, 207 (Drew); B 351, f. 33 (Reid); Booth, *Life and Labour*, Religious Influences, vol. 2, pp. 7, 15. See also, Russell and Lewis, *The Jew in London*, pp. 13-15; Feldman, *Englishmen and Jews*, p. 182.

[213] Booth, *Life and Labour*, Religious Influences, vol. 2, p. 7; Potter, "The Jewish Community", pp. 169-72, 189-91; Russell and Lewis, *The Jew in London*, pp. 60, 96, 101; Englander, "Jewish East London", p. 198.

(sic) moral bill than they deserve", citing the frequency of wife-desertion in evidence. Against this opinion, Inspector Barker of the Bethnal Green police division set the view that Jewish women were "more respected by their husbands & more faithful."[214] Undisputed was the fact that Jewish women withdrew from the workforce after marriage. This fact and the religious and ethnic traditions concerning hygiene, food preparation, diet, and breast-feeding seem to have contributed to the strikingly lower rate of infant mortality among the Jewish poor than that of neighbours living in similar socio-economic circumstances. Jewish children were in better health than Gentile children of the same age from the same districts. And they were more likely to attend school than non-Jewish children. Those leaving Berner Street board school in Whitechapel, close to where Elizabeth Stride was murdered by the Ripper, were described as "all clean, well fed, booted, large majority with hats ..." They were also expected to be obedient to parents and well behaved. As Willy Goldman testified, "Our parents continually reminded us: 'One bad Jew gets the whole race into trouble.'" Home life was also thought to underpin the sobriety of adult Jews. Both Willy Goldman and Emanuel Litvinoff believed the pub marked "the fundamentally different codes of our two peoples", the latter wisecracking, "a drunken Jew was as rare as a Yiddisher pork butcher." Superintendent Arnold of the Whitechapel police division agreed that it was "very seldom they are seen the worse for drink in the streets."[215]

---

[214] Booth Collection, Religious Influences Series, A 39 (8); Police Walks, B 352, f. 63 (Barker).

[215] Russell and Lewis, *The Jew in London*, p. 59; Hourwich, "The Jewish Laborer in London", pp. 90-92; M.W. Nevinson, *Life's Fitful Fever. A Volume of Memories* (London, 1926), p. 83; G. Black, "Health and medical care of the Jewish poor in the East End of London, 1880-1914", *Jewish Historical Studies*, vol. 36 (1999), p. 107; Marks, *Model Mothers*, pp. 9, 74; Booth, *Life and Labour,* Religious Influences, vol. 2, p. 4; Booth, *Life and Labour*, Final Volume, p. 74; Booth Collection, A 39(8), f. 15; Feldman, *Englishmen and Jews*, p. 252; Police Walks, B 350, f. 113 (Drew); W. Goldman, *East End My Cradle*, p. 21; E. Litvinoff, *Journey Through a Small Planet* (London, 1972), p. 66; NA, MEPO 2/ 260, Report by Supt. Arnold, 6 June 1888.

A Group of Jewish Children

When in need, Jews were prepared to take advantage of the community-sponsored services that were available. The *shtiblach*, or small synagogue rooms, were used to organize the collection of dues for payment in case of incapacity, old age, or sickness. The local health services were more than adequate and put to good use. As Gerry Black remarked: "If you had to be Jewish, poor and ill, the East End was a good place to be." In addition to London Hospital, there were numerous infirmaries, medical missions, and maternity services. Jews also applied for poor law relief, although the percentage of aliens relieved in 1901 at 3.9 per cent was half that of the total London population. The lower figure was due, in part, to the fact that the Jewish Board of Guardians also provided outdoor relief, and at a rather higher scale of payment. The Board, established in 1859, was an expression of private not state benevolence, and indeed the Jewish community was well served by its Anglo-Jewish philanthropists, who wanted to ensure that the 'pauper alien' did not bring disrepute on the community. The Board combined outdoor relief with other forms of assistance, including small business loans, apprenticeships, emigration, and repatriation (returning over 30,000 Jews who applied to them for poor relief to Europe between 1881 and 1906). It was active also in sanitary inspection of housing (pressing landlords to make repairs), health visiting, slum clearance and rebuilding. Philanthropists also worked to reduce crime and rehabilitate the fallen: the Hayes industrial school for Jewish boys, opened in 1901; Charcroft House rescue home in Mile End, opened by the Jewish Association for the Protection of Girls and Women.[216]

The argument is that the law-abidingness of the East End Jewish quarter was a function less of external policing and much more of the Jewish capacity for collective organization and the efforts of the Anglo-Jewry to help their co-religionists. Membership of the Jewish community meant a distinct set of values, ways of perceiving, and group reinforcement of beliefs and mores. Ethnic institutional support provided religious, recreational, and economic services without recourse to the host society. Ethnic leaders guided the attitudes and behaviour of group members. Once again, self- or internal 'policing' appears to be the effective factor.

XI

In the "economy of makeshift", survival depended not only upon the networks of kin and neighbourhood, but also upon private charity, both religious and secular. Family and welfare were

[216] Black, "Health and medical care", pp. 95, 103, 108; Booth, *Life and Labour*, Religious Influences, vol. 2, p. 9; *Royal Commission on Alien Immigration*, Evidence PP. 1903 [Cd. 1742], vol. IX, Appendix XXXI: Number of Aliens to whom Poor Law Relief was granted; L. Marks, "'The Luckless Waifs and Strays of Humanity:' Irish and Jewish Immigrant Unwed Mothers in London, 1870-1939", *Twentieth Century British History*. Vol. 3 (1992), pp. 122-24; Potter, "The Jewish Community", p. 173; A. Gillie, "The origin of the poverty line", *Economic History Review*, vol. XLIX (1996), note 19, p. 717; Marks, *Model Mothers*, pp. 34-5; W.J. Ashley, "Booth's East London", *Political Science Quarterly*, vol. 5 (1890), p. 518; Lipman, *Social Service*, p. 123; Feldman, *Englishmen and Jews*, pp. 156, 252, 303; D. Feldman, "Jews in London, 1880-1914", in R. Samuel (ed.), *Patriotism: The Making and Unmaking of British National Identity*, vol. 2 (London, 1989), pp. 214, 222; Feldman, "The importance of being English", in Feldman and Jones, *Metropolis-London*, pp. 65-66.

complementary resources in the household economy of the East End poor. Studies of many parts of London have concluded that the charitable and social services that churches provided their parishioners were more effective than other aspects of the churches' work. This role would contract in the early twentieth century as the state and local government increasingly assumed responsibility for welfare and education. But at the time of Booth's survey, the churches were still making heroic efforts via numerous relief and social programs to attack the apathy and irreligiosity of the London working classes. Not all clergymen were eager to satisfy the exclusively material demands of their flock. The Rev. Richard Free from the Isle of Dogs had to admit that the parson, "as philanthropist-in-chief, is 'the soup-ticket man', and he has himself to blame if he is little else. He has done his best to spoil the East-ender, in whose estimation he is half knave, half fool." Many other clergymen and district visitors warned against indiscriminate charity, but church workers continued to dish it out; the spigot stayed open.[217] Our focus now turns to the contribution of these charitable and state agencies to the survival of the working poor. It is a story of welfare clients as active, reflexive agents, negotiating for resources, "foraging" (to use Arthur Harding's term for his mother's coping strategy), and shaping the nature of the social welfare experience.[218]

---

[217] R. Free, *Seven Years' Hard* (New York, 1905), p. 227; H. McCleod, *Piety and Poverty. Working-Class Religion in Berlin, London and New York 1870-1914* (New York, 1996), p. 47; idem., "Working-class religion in late Victorian London: Booth's 'Religious Influences' revisited", in Englander and O'Day, *Retrieved Riches*, pp. 269-70; J. Cox, *The English Churches in a Secular Society* (Oxford, 1982), passim. See also August, *The British Working Class*, p. 156; E. Ross (ed.), *Slum Travelers. Ladies and London Poverty, 1860-1920* (Berkeley, 2007), p. 4.

[218] Brydon, "Charles Booth, Charity Control", pp. 494, 517-18; Jones, "The 'cockney' and the nation", p. 306; R. O'Day, "Caring or Controlling? The East End of London in the 1880s and 1890s", in C. Emsley et al (eds.), *Social Control in Europe 1800-2000* (Columbia, 2004), vol. 2, pp. 149, 153, 163; L. Murdoch, *Imagined Orphans. Poor Families, Child Welfare, and Contested Citizenship in London* (New Brunswick, 2006), pp. 7-8. By contrast to the work so far cited, Susan Pennybacker's analysis is much less nuanced. She describes the relations between the advocates of urban welfare and their subjects as a straightforward example of social control, not as a

Duckworth's report on Hackney expresses best the important role of the churches on the front line of survival. He divided the working poor into two groups: the first consisting of Booth's classes E, F, and a good few of class D, the respectable working class, 10 per cent of whom were sincere churchgoers; the second group consisting of classes A, B, C, and some of D, "scarcely ever churchgoers except for the loaves and fishes, but with their lives touched on every side by the social and philanthropic activities of the religious bodies." The poorer the population, said Duckworth, "the more likely is it to be in close touch with the church." Artisans and labourers alike sent their children to Sunday Schools (with some churches providing separate services for rough and respectable children), but otherwise "the churches scarcely touch the life of the respectable non-church going working class at any point." "[T]he very poor on the other hand are constantly leaning on the Churches: they are visited (usually by several agencies) & relieved, nursed, amused, brought into clubs, mother' meetings, penny banks, temperance societies etc. to such an extent that it is safe to say that among them there is scarcely a family in the life of which the religious agencies fail to play an important part." Booth himself appended two other observations in the same vein. To the poor, "none are Greeks, and all may be welcomed who bring gifts." Among "the quite rough poor", the women soaked up the charity on offer, "and take relief and religion as they come. On them depends the keeping of the home together, by what they earn or what they beg."[219]

As well as helping with material survival, the churches added to the refinement of working class life, however marginally. The Rev. Lawley, former vicar of St. Andrew's in Bethnal Green, claimed he had 1,000 children at Sunday School

---

flexible dialogue: A *Vision for London 1889-1914* (London, 1995). Indeed, the rich history of the LCC deserved far better than this opaquely-argued and maladroitly-written book.

[219] Booth Collection, Notebooks on the Religious Influences Series, A 35 (i), ff. 49-51; Booth, *Life and Labour*, Religious Influences, vol. 1, pp. 81, 85. See also Samuel, *East End Underworld*, note 4, p. 295.

each week. Boys clubs and brigades supplemented the meagre facilities for adolescent recreation. Lawley also claimed that one Bethnal Green district had been civilized mainly through the mothers' meeting, which taught household virtues. "It was a district of free family fights. Always a row on between warlike mothers. In 3 years this was altered." The churches were also used for occasional conformity to such rituals as baptism, marriage, churching (for the mother coming out for the first time after giving birth), and funerals.[220]

Secular charity was no less active than the churches in the East End, and again, as Ellen Ross argued, this charity supplied "a surprisingly large proportion of the resources on which poor people drew", and was considered to be "a neigbourhood resource."[221] Potential recipients adopted the required deferential pose, in what Mandler called "the theatre of charity", but they took the materialism without the moralism. The trick was to look "deserving". The Report on Mile End Old Town for the Booth survey spoke of "the perfect deluge of charitable relief which pours from District 10; and which no doubt overflows ... into the surrounding districts." The Great Assembly Hall, the East London Tabernacle, and Edinburgh Castle gave teas, dinners and other forms of relief. And it was not just District 10. Booth intimated that the association in the public mind of poverty, destitution and depravity with the 'East End' had led to this part of London receiving much more than its fair share of assistance. Philanthropic attention was focused in particular on

---

[220] Police Walks, B 350, ff. 120, 122; S.C. Williams, "Urban Popular Religion and the Rites of Passage", in H. McCleod (ed.), *European Religion in the Age of Great Cities 1830-1930* (London, 1995), pp. 219, 230; idem., "The Problem of Belief: The Place of Oral History in the Study of Popular Religion", *Oral History*, vol. 24 (1996), p. 31; Free, *Seven Years' Hard*, p. 247; Booth Collection, A 32 (i), f. 19. See also F. Prochaska, *Christianity and Social Service in Modern Britain* (Oxford, 2006), pp. 22-3. Churches and settlements institutionalized the rough/respectable division in the services they provided: Ross, "Respectability", p. 43.

[221] Ross, "Survival Networks", pp. 19-20; Ross, "Hungry Children: Housewives and London Charity, 1870-1918", in P. Mandler (ed.), *The Uses of Charity. The Poor on Relief in the Nineteenth Century Metropolis* (Philadelphia, 1990), p. 161.

semi-criminal areas like the Nichol in Bethnal Green, but the respectable working class in the Rothschild Buildings in Spitalfields were the beneficiaries of a dozen societies and clubs that provided soup, dinners, shoes, clothing holidays, and medical assistance. One of the most widespread forms of charity was the medical assistance provided by voluntary hospitals and district nurses. The latter could walk the streets in the poorest areas without fear of attack. In the case of Dr. Barnardo's homes for destitute children, which Booth trumpeted as "the greatest charitable institution in London", admissions were typically the result of a severe family crisis and a breakdown in the tradition of mutual assistance.[222]

So far we have assessed the 'mixed economy' of welfare in its family and voluntary — both religious and secular — capacities. To this we need to add the state in the form of the Poor Law, since the vicarage, soup kitchen, dispensary and workhouse were all integral to what David Englander called "the

---

[222] August, "A culture of consolation", p. 203; Johnson, "Private and Public Social Welfare", p. 146; Prochaska, *Christianity and Social Service*, p. 67; Booth Collection, A 33(i), f. 31; A 33(i), f. 13; Ross, *Love and Toil*, p. 173; Booth, *Life and Labour*, Religious Influences, vol. 2, p. 46; Davin, *Growing Up Poor*, p. 60. The Charity Organization Society also had a presence in the East End. From its foundation in 1869, the Society rejected the practice of indiscriminate charity, on the grounds that the poor needed to learn economic foresight. Aid should be withheld from those for whom there was no hope of economic independence. Only the 'deserving' or respectable poor were to be helped, undeserving paupers were to be forwarded to the Poor Law. Voluntary social work within the C.O.S. was a largely female world. Women like Octavia Hill taught women like Beatrice Webb how to raise the standards of housekeeping and behaviour in the homes and buildings they visited. The response of the poor was largely hostile. John Galt of the London City Mission in Poplar said the Society was hated because of the "brutal impudence" of the women visitors. And the numbers helped were small. Applicants for relief to the C.O.S. in St. George's and Mile End Old Town between October 1887 and September 1888 numbered fewer than 700: Booth Collection, B 172, f. 9; K. Furse, *Hearts and Pomegranates. The Story of Forty-five years 1875-1920* (London, 1940), p. 156 (Furse worked in a COS office in Whitechapel); P. Thompson, *Socialists, Liberals and Labour. The Struggle for London 1885-1914* (London, 1967), p. 22.

social economy of the poor."[223] Booth recognized that successful efforts had been made in the East End since 1870 to reduce outdoor relief without a corresponding increase in indoor pauperism. The Whitechapel, St. George's and Stepney Unions sought to instill independence and raise living standards by decreasing the amount of assistance to the outdoor poor. Less than seven per cent of the relief granted in these Unions was outdoor relief. In Stepney Union, where most men were employed on the wharves and docks, the number of outdoor poor fell from 7602 in 1869 to 177 in 1890. Indeed, the people helped by the poor law in Stepney on January 1, 1891, in all possible forms, made up only 1.5 per cent of the total population. Booth was not convinced by the results of this experiment: "The people are no less poor, nor much, if at all, more independent. There are fewer paupers, but not fewer who rely on charity in some form." Alongside the crusade against out relief, however, went the improvement of the treatment of the sick in poor law infirmaries. In Bethnal Green, meanwhile, both indoor and outdoor pauperism had grown, "the numbers relieved and the amount expended being more than double in 1895 what they were in 1878."[224] And between 1892 and 1895, unemployed demonstrations on Tower Hill and the riverside districts prompted some boards of guardians to provide stone breaking work.[225]

What of those who resorted to indoor relief or the workhouse? What is evident from the findings of Lynn Hollen Lees and David Englander is that a significant proportion of the London population, notably women, children and the aged, applied for relief, so the poor law was "a familiar and accepted donor of services", and that the poor exploited workhouse shelter, sick asylums, and boarding schools on their own terms to

---

[223] Englander, "Research Note: From the Abyss: Pauper Petitions and Correspondence in Victorian London", *London Journal*, vol. 25 (2000), p. 81.

[224] Booth, *Life and Labour*, Poverty, vol. 1, p. 129; Industry, vol. 4, p. 312; Religious Influences, vol. 2, pp. 51-2. See also Ross, "Survival Networks", note 110, p. 27.

[225] L.H. Lees, *The Solidarities of Strangers. The English Poor Laws and the People, 1700-1948* (Cambridge, 1998), p. 291.

surmount short-term, life cycle crises. Most of the paupers in Stepney institutions, said Lees, "had come there by their own or their family's choice", in the absence of more palatable alternatives. East End paupers saw themselves, said Englander, "as people with rights", who expected to return to family and friends once the crisis had passed. Not for them the social exclusion that poor law principles intended. East End prostitute, Frances Coles, Englander tells us, "regularly visited her inmate father before her throat was cut in a Jack-the-Ripper-style attack in 1891."[226] The state poor law was thus an added resource in the mixed economy of welfare for the East End working classes.

XII

Duckworth was always willing to take an independent line in his work for the Booth survey. "'I have placed religion last because though it takes the first place in our evidence I believe that on the whole it plays a less important part in the lives of the people than either education or government activity, whether central or local.'"[227] This section of the study investigates the impact of schools and local authorities on the material well-being and social conduct of the East End working classes. In time, Booth followed Duckworth's lead: "the indirect disciplinary influence of the school is far greater than that of the Churches and Missions." Indeed, for Booth, the Board Schools were surrogate churches: "Each school stands up from its playground like a church in God's acre ringing its bell."[228]

---

[226] Lees, *Solidarities*, pp. 281-87; Booth, *Life and Labour*, Industry, vol. 4, pp. 393-473; L.H. Lees, "The Survival of the Unfit: Welfare Policies and Family Maintenance in Nineteenth-Century London", in P. Mandler (ed.), *The Uses of Charity. The Poor on Relief in the Nineteenth Century Metropolis* (Philadelphia, 1990), pp. 69-70, 82, 85-6; Englander, "Research Note", pp. 77, 80-81.

[227] Booth Collection, A 37, f. 64.

[228] Booth, *Life and Labour*, Religious Influences, p. 52; Poverty, vol. 1, p. 129. Arthur Conan Doyle has Sherlock Holmes describe the Board Schools as "'Lighthouses, my Boy! Beacons of the future! ... out of which will spring the wiser, better England of the future:'" "The Naval Treaty", in *The Penguin Complete Sherlock Holmes* (London, 1981), pp. 456-7. See also A. Jackson,

Of two things we can be sure: London was "a city of children", particularly in the poorest districts; and officially recorded juvenile crime was declining yet still pervasive. In 1871, 43 per cent of the London population was aged fifteen or under; by 1901 this had fallen to just under one-third. In the East London boroughs of Shoreditch and Bethnal Green, however, the 1901 figure was 36 and 38 per cent respectively. Amongst all London boroughs, fertility rates declined least in Bethnal Green, Stepney, Shoreditch, and Poplar. Not surprisingly, East End streets and courts were full of children from morning till night.[229] The national figures of juvenile delinquency indicate that between 1893 and 1905, indictable crime amongst those aged 12 to 16 fell from 261 to 218 per 100,000 people of this age group. Yet juvenile crime remained significant, since one-fifth of all convicted larcenists and one-quarter of those convicted specifically of picking pockets in the 1890s were aged under 16, despite the fact that some 17 per cent of juvenile offenders in London were discharged without conviction though the charges had been proved, under section 16(1) of the Summary Jurisdiction Act, 1879, and many thousands who were either criminals or in danger of becoming so were confined in industrial schools.[230]

It was in this setting that the Board Schools sprang up after the 1870 Education Act. Children aged 5 to 10 (raised to 11 in 1893) had to attend school full-time unless they were chronically ill; those between 10 and 13 could be "half-timers" if it could be proved the child's employment was crucial to family survival. In the last quarter of the nineteenth century, school

"'Sermons in Brick': Design and Social Purpose in London Board Schools", *London Journal*, vol. 18 (1993), pp. 42-3.

[229] Ross, *Slum Travelers*, note 6, p. 285; Ross, *Love and Toil*, p. 13; note 6, p. 229.

[230] Radzinowicz and Hood, *History of Criminal Law*, vol. 5, pp. 119; *Departmental Committee on Prisons*, PP 1895 [c.7702-I], Evidence, Appendices, p. 541: Proportion of Young Offenders in different classes of crime; Gatrell, "Decline", p. 305 and note 125; J. Holt Schooling, "Crime. Part III", *The Pall Mall Magazine*, vol. XVI (1898), p. 109.

became the experience of most children.[231] The attendance rate varied from school to school. By 1900, in Whitechapel and Bethnal Green, the thirty-seven Board Schools were returning an 81 per cent attendance rate, with truancy running at 20 per cent. The highest truancy rates were to be found amongst girls, whose mothers needed their domestic service and against whom attendance officers were less vigilant, and in the poorest London schools. Booth highlighted one poor Board school in Bethnal Green, where the children's fathers were costers and fish-curers, which had an attendance under 70 per cent. Booth's police guides singled out the Irish as the worst truants. In Hoxton Square, the Catholic schools were poorly attended, the distance from the homes being so far. In the Fenian Barracks, the children "used not to go to school at all, and are no doubt very irregular still, but the Sisters now 'go to fetch them and often wash and dress them.'" In a cockney Irish area of Shadwell, Inspector Drew and Duckworth came upon three barefoot boys who cried "here's the School Board", and disappeared.[232]

Yet if a sizeable group of children played truant, it is hard to deny that the schools did an effective job of uprooting at-risk children from the temptations of the street. Speaking of the "street arabs" of East London in 1889, Booth declared, "[s]ome are in the Board schools, and more in ragged schools, and the remainder, who cannot be counted, and may still be numerous, are every year confined within narrowing bounds by the persistent pressure of the School Board and other agencies."[233] An ancillary benefit of schooling was the reduction

---

[231] Davin, *Growing Up Poor*, p. 10; D. Rubinstein, "Socialization and the London School Board 1870-1904: aims, methods and public opinion", in P. McCann (ed.), *Popular education and socialization in the nineteenth century* (London, 1977), 232.

[232] Booth, *Life and Labour*, Final Volume, pp. 222-23; Davin, *Growing Up Poor*, p. 110; *Life and Labour*, Religious Influences, vol. 2, pp. 129, 241; vol. 1, p. 48; Police Walks, B 350, f. 215 (Drew). See also H.B. Philpott, *London at School. The Story of the School Board, 1870-1904* (London, 1904), p. 299.

[233] Booth, *Life and Labour*, Poverty, vol. 1, pp. 38-9. See also Gatrell, "Decline", p. 307.

in the size of the juvenile labour pool, which could only improve the bargaining position of teenage boy labour.[234]

The job of building support for the new schools fell to attendance officers, colloquially known as "School Board men." Most were from working-class backgrounds, many were former soldiers or policemen. In the early years, attendance officers were met with conflict and confrontation, but parental opposition slowly subsided, and the officers had an easier time with the second generation of elementary scholars. Their work was doubtless helped by the provision of free meals. During the harsh winter of 1895, one-tenth of the children, or 52,000, on London board school rolls were fed two to three meals in one February week. Likewise, Booth reported: "At most schools in poor districts, and that applies to nearly all the schools here [Whitechapel and St, George's], free breakfasts and dinners are arranged when required for necessitous children." For the most part, attendance officers persuaded and cajoled parents to send their children to school. Occasionally, all the officers of a division would participate in a dragnet of the streets to question children they found there during school hours. And the police court, finally, was used to bring intractable parents and children into line. Thousands of parents were prosecuted for failing to send their children regularly to school. Persistent truants were sent to truant school for a month or more. In the Orchard House area of Poplar "[t]here is no family", said Booth, "which has not had a child sent by the magistrate's order to a truant school." By 1898, there were 400 children in the East End Industrial Schools whose truancy was aggravated by homelessness, criminal associations, or being out of parental control.[235]

---

[234] Jones, *Outcast London*, p. 72.

[235] The Poverty volumes of the Booth survey relied heavily on the School Board Visitors, since they possessed such an intimate knowledge of working-class life. P. Gardner, "'Our Schools'; 'their schools.' The case of Eliza Duckworth and John Stevenson", *History of Education*, vol. 20 (1991), pp. 165-67; D. Rubinstein, *School Attendance in London, 1870-1904: A Social History* (Hull, 1969), pp. 42, 44, 53; E. Ross, "Hungry Children: Housewives and London Charity, 1870-1918", in Mandler (ed.), *The Uses of Charity*, p. 176; Philpott, *London At School*, pp. 88-90, 189, 296; Booth, *Life and Labour*,

By the end of the century, Booth had no doubt about "the general civilizing influences of the schools." It was less the knowledge imparted than the socialization of children that he and his informants emphasized. An assistant teacher at Summerford Street school in Bethnal Green spoke of a pronounced change in "the whole demeanour of the native born child." He asked rhetorically: "Where are the rebels and outlaws and young villains of a dozen years ago? The school has not existed for nothing." Booth underlined the formation of habits of cleanliness and order, of dress and decency, of the difference between right and wrong. And he concluded: "Obedience to discipline and rules of proper behaviour have been inculcated; habits of order and cleanliness have been acquired; and from these habits self-respect arises."[236] This could not fail to react upon the homes. School officials expected working-class mothers to elevate their standards of care in terms of health, cleanliness and dress.[237] State education, in short, helped to render the East End populace law-abiding and conformist for the next half century.

Canon Barnett once famously stated: "There is very little of what can be called Local Government in East London. The Boards are not in touch with the people." He was referring to the

---

Religious Influences, vol. 1, p. 50; vol. 2, p. 48; Police Walks, B 352, f. 61 (Barker); J. Martin, "'Hard-headed and large-hearted': women and the industrial schools, 1870-1885", *History of Education,* vol. 20 (1991), pp. 193-4; Clementina Black, "Labour and Life in London", *Contemporary Review,* vol. LX (1891), p. 211.

[236] Booth, *Life and Labour,* Religious Influences, vol. 1, p. 17; vol. 2, pp. 53-55; W.E. Marsden, "Charles Booth and the social geography of education in late nineteenth-century London", in Englander and O'Day, *Retrieved Riches,* p. 259; idem., "Education and the Social Geography of Nineteenth-Century Towns and Cities", in D.A. Reeder (ed.), *Urban Education in the Nineteenth Century* (New York, 1978), p. 72; idem, "Residential Segregation and the Hierarchy of Elementary Schooling", *London Journal,* vol. 11 (1985), p. 141; Davin, *Growing Up Poor,* p. 134; Mary C. Tabor, "Elementary Education", in Booth, *Life and Labour,* Poverty, vol. 3, p. 211; Booth, *Life and Labour,* Final Volume, p. 202. See also McKibbin, "Class and Poverty", pp. 186-7. Of course, not everyone agreed that schools were a force for good: J. Greenwood, *The Prisoner in the Dock* (London, 1902), p. 41.

[237] Ross, "Respectability", p. 40; Davin, *Growing Up Poor,* p. 133.

parish vestries, composed largely of penny-pinching tradesmen, supervising health and sanitation, which were grouped into District Boards of Works. The population of Whitechapel, Limehouse, and Poplar, he continued, "lived under the dead hand of the District Board System."[238] As a result, the lighting, water supply, sanitation, and street maintenance in the East End left a lot to be desired. In 1900, borough councils replaced the vestries. More importantly, a popularly-elected authority, the London County Council, was established in 1889 as the main governmental authority. While the Council's regulations were honoured more in the breach than the observance, the Council worked hard to protect children under five in paid care, deter shopkeepers from using illegal child labour, supervise lodging houses (a task they inherited from the metropolitan police in 1894), regulate street trading, and clear parks of vagrants and prostitutes, music halls of prostitutes. Indeed, the L.C.C. became part of the larger movement to purify metropolitan life.[239]

For present purposes, the most important campaign of local government (plus private philanthropy) was the clearance of slum property and its replacement by new and model dwellings. This physical restructuring of London destroyed some of the worst environments of the semi-criminal poor. Booth remarked that in the East End the sites of board schools were purposely chosen; "the clearance for the school-house has been made very often in the midst of the worst class of property." The opium den in Limehouse Walk that Dickens described in *Edwin Drood* made way for one new board school. The most extensive clearances of insanitary and overcrowded housing were the result of railway expansion, the spread of City warehouses, and local government initiative.[240]

---

[238] Cited in J. Davis, *Reforming London*, note 55, p. 232.

[239] See Davies, *Reforming London*, pp. 18, 23, 40, 232; Ross, *Love and Toil*, p. 13; S. Pennybacker, "Reconsidering London Progressivism", in Feldman and Jones, *Metropolis-London*, p. 131; Pennybacker, *Vision*, pp. 174-6; C. Waters, "Progressives, Puritans and the Cultural Politics of the Council, 1889-1914", in A. Saint (ed.), *Politics and the People of London* (London, 1989), pp. 50, 59, 61-2, 65.

[240] Booth cited in Marsden, "Residential Segregation", p. 141; H. Llewellyn

Re-building on slum clearance sites was the mission largely of "philanthropy at five per cent", which built "model" block dwellings. In 1885, Katharine Buildings was erected by the East End Dwellings Company on a site in Cartwright Street, close to the Tower of London. In Spitalfields, the warrens of Flower and Dean Street and Thrawl Street were torn down and replaced by the Charlotte de Rothschild dwellings. Peabody buildings went up in Shadwell. However, the most ambitious scheme belonged to the London County Council, which 'scheduled' thirteen acres of the worst Bethnal Green slum, renowned as a forcing-house of crime, for the building of the Boundary Street Estate in the 1890s.[241]

It is by now accepted wisdom that most of the inhabitants of these areas were not re-housed in "model" dwellings; rather, they crowded into neighbouring streets or migrated to other districts. Less than five per cent of the original inhabitants could afford to live in the Boundary Street Estate. Only eleven of the close to 6,000 evicted Nichol residents lived on the Estate. Booth himself estimated that 60 per cent of the 190,000 inhabitants of "models" were from classes E and F, or the well-to-do working class. Less than 10 per cent were from classes A and B, or the very poor, even though model blocks were typically built on sites from which these classes had been ejected.

Smith, "Influx of Population", in Booth, *Life and Labour*, Poverty, vol. 3, p. 101; Poverty, vol. 1, p. 69. See also P.T. Smith, *Policing Victorian London* (Westport, 1985), p. 207. In the 1880s, the clearances occurred principally in Whitechapel and St. George's, while a large number of lodging houses were pulled down in the Wentworth Street neighbourhood in Spitalfields.
[241] Dennis, *Cities in Modernity*, p. 70; Waters, "Progressives", p. 57; W.J Fishman, *Jewish Radicals* (New York, 1975), p. 58; J. White, "Jewish Landlords, Jewish Tenants", in *The Jewish East End*, p. 213; J. Walkowitz, "Jack the Ripper", p. 569; Brodie, *Politics of the Poor*, pp. 110-11; A. Newsholme, "The Vital Statistics of Peabody Buildings and other Artisans' and Labourers' Block Dwellings", *Journal of the Royal Statistical Society*, vol. 54 (1891), pp 72-3. Newsholme revealed that the Peabody Buildings housed a high proportion of persons under 15 years of age, and that infantile mortality was much lower in the Buildings than for the entire city, and especially for St. George's-in-the-East.

Rents were too high and earnings too irregular for the casual poor to find permanent homes in block dwellings. The blocks owned by philanthropic societies were weighted even more heavily against classes A to D, or the very poor and poor. The odd one out was Katharine Buildings, which was intended for Booth's class B. The numbers housed in these block buildings continued to rise, however. By the end of the century, some 16,000 out of a total Whitechapel population of 80,000, or 20 per cent, were housed in block dwellings. Even higher percentages were to be found in parts of Shadwell and Wapping.[242]

The results of slum clearance and rehousing were mixed, to say the least. The Boundary Street Estate brought no improvement to the lives of the poor. Katharine Buildings, with their "uniform cell-like apartments", were, said rent collector Beatrice Webb, "an utter failure ... they are not an influence for good." Yet there were gains. The Rothschild Buildings filled up with "poor, but respectable Jews", who built, according to Fiona Rule, "a strong sense of community and mutual support ... and the tenement rules (which looked very forbidding on paper) were generally enforced by the tenants themselves in the interests of safe and orderly communal living."[243] Booth's police informants maintained that, where the rules were lax, no worse places existed, but that buildings with strong caretakers, according to Superintendent Weston of Bethnal Green, "do more to humanize a rough neighbourhood than 'all the Churches, chapels & missions put together.' 'What that class want is discipline & a

---

[242] Wise, *The Blackest Streets*, pp. 265-66; Dennis, *Cities in Modernity*, pp. 250-52; Booth, *Life and Labour*, Religious Influences, vol. 2, pp. 59, 68, 71; Police Walks, B 350, f. 227 (Drew on Wapping).

[243] Webb, *My Apprenticeship*, p. 282; J. Green, *A Social History of the Jewish East End of London 1914-1939* (Lewiston, 1991), p. 245; R. Livesey, "Women Rent Collectors and the Rewriting of Space, Class and Gender in East London, 1870-1900", in E. Darling and L. Whitworth (eds.), *Women and the Making of Built Space in England, 1870-1950* (Aldershot, 2007); P. Townsend, SN 4756, Katharine Buildings, 1885-1962, Fieldwork 1957-62, National Social Policy and Social Change Archive, University of Essex Economic and Social Data Service; Rule, *The Worst Street in London*, pp. 90-1; White, *Rothschild Buildings*, pp. 24-5.

sense of orderliness introduced into their lives.'" P. C. Machell from Old Street observed, "'we very rarely get any of the criminal class from model dwellings.'" As for the overall impact of clearance and re-building, Booth and his team had no doubts. Ernest Aves's report on Bethnal Green acknowledged that streets surrounding the Boundary Street Estate had suffered, "but the community as a whole gains from this wholesale ejection of large numbers of the 'submerged.'" Booth added that in this neighbourhood brutality had diminished. "Thieving still is an every-day offence, and burglary not unknown, but crimes of violence have become more rare." Booth also quoted the view of one informant on the impact on the character of the inhabitants of Whitechapel and St. George's: "'As poor as ever, but old rookeries destroyed, black patches cleared away, thieves and prostitutes gone, a marvellous change for the better.'"[244]

XIII

In *The Adventure of the Copper Beeches*, novelist Arthur Conan Doyle described the role of public opinion in setting the law in motion. "There is no lane so vile that the scream of a tortured child, or the thud of a drunkard's blow, does not beget sympathy and indignation among the neighbours, and then the whole machinery of justice is ever so close that a word of complaint can set it going, and there is but a step between the crime and the dock."[245] His words introduce the final dimension in the neighbourhood dynamic, the mutual relations of the people, the police (including the 'family police' of truancy and child protection officers), and the police courts (which despite the name were independent of the police).

[244] Police Walks, B 350, f. 40 (Weston); B 350, f. 81 (Drew); B 353, f. 65 (Machell); Booth Collection, Religious Influences Series, A 39, f. 7 (Aves); Booth, *Life and Labour*, Religious Influences, vol. 3, p. 84; vol. 2, p. 61. Louise Jackson claimed that the replacement of lodging-houses with model dwellings led to a reduction in prostitution in Whitechapel: "Law, Order and Violence", in Werner, *Jack the Ripper*, p. 122.
[245] Conan Doyle, "The Adventure of the Copper Beeches", in *The Penguin Complete Sherlock Holmes*, p 323.

The entire system of summary justice in London was in the hands of two-dozen stipendiary magistrates, who wielded considerable discretion. Two police courts served the East End, Worship Street court (later Old Street), serving the northern part of Whitechapel, Spitalfields, Shoreditch and Bethnal Green (including the rookeries of Flower and Dean Street, and the Nichol); and Thames court, serving the southern limits of Whitechapel, Stepney, Limehouse, and Poplar (including the London Docks). Albert Cluer and Montagu Williams presided at Worship Street police court; Frederick Mead and John Dickenson at Thames police court. The police court was the clearing-house of crime, as ever more indictable offences were dealt with summarily, and as all non-indictable prosecutions began and ended there. By 1900, 81 per cent of all criminal offences in London were adjudicated summarily. Magistrates dealt with a host of urban disputes and offences: tenancy wrangles, school truancy, attempted suicide, domestic violence, assaults, vagrancy, drunkenness, gambling, and petty theft. Only a small fraction of cases were sent for trial to the higher courts.[246]

The police courts were much more than legal tribunals. As Jennifer Davis and others have shown, London magistrates were deeply involved in the life of the neighbourhood, and served both the interests of the state and the needs of their working-class clientele. William Fitzsimmons, who worked for twenty years as a court missionary at the Thames police court, described the role of the stipendiaries to the Royal Commission on Divorce. "They sit in the morning as poor man's lawyer, and give legal advice; they are really friends of the poor, and are trusted by them. They have their confidence. Their advice is sought on a thousand and one subjects ... They have intimate knowledge of the lives of the poor."[247]

---

[246] F.T. Giles, *The Magistrates' Courts* (London, 1949), p. 8; G. Behlmer, *Friends of the Family. The English Home and Its Guardians, 1850-1940* (Stanford, 1998), p. 183; A. Lieck, *Bow Street World* (London, 1938), pp. 32, 73-4; Leeson, *Lost London*, p. 96 (for Thames magistrates); E.B. Conway, "London's Police Courts", in G. Sims (ed.), *Living London* (London, 1901), vol 2, p. 141.

[247] *Report of the Royal Commission on Divorce and Matrimonial Causes,*

No day in court was entirely representative, but on the morning of August 18, 1890, Montagu Williams at Worship Street court dealt with 31 applications for summons and 36 charges. Eight of the 31 summons were requested by women whose husbands were violent; two by women who needed child maintenance. Six summons were requested by those who said they had been assaulted (three of the six were male-on-male; one was male-on-female; and two were female-on-female violence). Three involved labour issues (discharging workers without notice); two involved rental issues (lodgers owing rent); two involved tenancy agreements; and eight involved miscellaneous issues (a foreign Jew whose window was broken by a woman, a woman complaining that her son had been sent to a reformatory, and a man who wanted admission to the workhouse). Of the 36 charges that came before Williams, 19 or just over half were for offences resulting from intoxication (drunk and disorderly offences); six were for assault (three for assault on a policeman, three for assault on a wife); six were for gambling (almost all young boys); the remaining five for crimes against property (embezzlement, housebreaking, and stealing from stalls). The penalties were hardly severe. Almost three-quarters (14 of the 19) of the drunk and disorderly offenders were discharged; the young gamblers, if unable to pay the fine of five shillings, were discharged at the end of the afternoon. Only those assaulting the police or stealing from stalls got sent to prison.[248]

The picture was similar in the Thames police court. Figures from three summer months in 1888 indicate that of the 2,174 defendants, 30 per cent of cases involved minor public

---

Evidence [Cd. 6480], PP. 1912-13, vol. XIX, q. 19,535 (Fitzsimmons). See also Gamon, *The London Police Court*, p. 231; H.T. Waddy, *The Police Court and Its Work* (London, 1925), p. 4; C. Chapman, *The Poor Man's Court of Justice: Twenty Five Years as a Metropolitan Magistrate* (London, n.d.), p. 12; Anderson, *Suicide*, p. 309. For examples of the varied duties of the police courts, see *Reynolds's Newspaper*, 12 Sept. 1897 ("Anxious to Marry"); *Lloyd's Weekly Newspaper*, 3 October 1897 ("Apprentices and the Lock-Out"); *Reynolds's Newspaper*, 12 June 1898 (Attempted Suicide).

[248] *Later Leaves. Being the Further Reminiscences of Montagu Williams, QC* (London, 1891), pp. 304-324.

order (mostly related to drunkenness), 27 per cent involved interpersonal violence (one-quarter of which were assaults on policeman; one quarter were cases of wife beating, and another quarter were female-on-female violence), 23 per cent concerned property (theft and receiving); and 20 per cent involved such offences as gambling, begging, and cruelty to animals. Women formed over one-quarter (27 per cent) of all defendants, notably for drink-related offences and common assault. Some days were different, namely when School Board summonses were taken; or at emergency sessions in the wake of bank holidays, and on 'Black Monday' each week, when above-average numbers were charged with drunkenness and disorderly conduct, and when aggrieved wives queued for summonses against their husbands.[249]

When it came to adjudicating disputes, the magistrates tried to do so with some regard to popular definitions of justice, willing to distinguish between the just and the narrowly legal. They also sought the help of prisoners' friends and families, and police court missionaries (who conducted pre-trial interviews), in deciding cases. They even offered relief from the court's poor box in individual cases of hardship and in times of distress. In all, the courts were a vital neighbourhood resource, which the working poor sought to exploit.[250]

Aggrieved women flocked to the police courts for help

---

[249] Jackson, "Law, Order and Violence", pp. 114-5, 118, 123-4; R.E. Corder, *Tales Told to the Magistrate* (London, 1925), p. 13. See also D. Gray, *London's Shadows. The Dark Side of the Victorian City* (London, 2010), pp. 175-81; M.C. Finn, "The Authority of the Law", in P. Mandler (ed.), *Liberty and Authority in Victorian Britain* (Oxford, 2006). See *Lloyd's Weekly Newspaper*, 2 April 1899 for "Good Friday Charges." For complaints about the indecent haste of police court business, see Timewell, *Police and Public*, pp. 2, 15; Leeson, *Lost London*, p. 63; Nevinson, *Life's Fitful Fever*, p. 94.

[250] Gatrell, "policeman-state", p. 282; J. Walkowitz, *City of Dreadful Delight* (Chicago, 1992), p. 109. *Hackney Gazette*, 30 May 1906: magistrate Albert Cluer stated in court: "Let the people come in ... It is absolutely essential that friends of the prisoners should hear the cases. ... Time and again have I been assisted by them in trying to deal out justice." Williams, *Round London* (in winter, 1891, he opened a depot for relief of distress in the Thames and Worship Street districts).

with violent or neglectful husbands, usually after more informal expedients had failed or as a coercive supplement to them. They had to pay two shillings for a summons, no small amount, unless physical evidence of violence moved the magistrate to grant a free summons. East End women were renowned for pressing their cases with gusto, if not always with brevity or logic. The courtroom provided an opportunity for women to present their side of the dispute.[251] At times, popular and legal opinion coincided. In January, 1898, before Mead at the Thames police court, a Stepney husband was charged with assaulting his wife; on conviction, he was sentenced to six weeks' hard labour. He had failed to respond to his wife's original summons, so a warrant had been issued for his apprehension. As the warrant officer arrested the prisoner, "a crowd was round the house hooting the prisoner." One imagines that the domestic assault cases that came to court were the most egregious ones, since fear of retaliation must have deterred many, if not most, women from seeking legal redress. When cases came to court, they were frequently dismissed because the wife failed to appear, or because magistrates chose an out-of-court settlement in order to preserve the marital bond.[252]

Other forms of interpersonal conflict in street and home were brought to the courts. The summons was a handy weapon in

---

[251] See M. May, "Violence in the Family: An Historical Perspective", in J.P. Martin (ed.), *Violence and the Family* (Chichester, 1979), p. 149; Ross, *Love and Toil*, p. 74; Behlmer, *Friends of the Family*, pp. 191-94; G. Savage, "'The Magistrates are Men': Working-Class Marital Conflict and Appeals from the Magistrates' Court to the Divorce Court after 1895", in G. Robb and N. Erber (eds.), *Disorder in the Court. Trials and Sexual Conflict at the Turn of the Century* (New York, 1999), pp. 232, 245; A. Martin, "The Mother and Social Reform", The *Nineteenth Century*, vol. 73 (1913), pp. 1075-6; Greenwood, *Prisoner in the Dock*, p. 14; Corder, *Tales Told*, p. 13; John Law (Margaret Harkness), *In Darkest London* (London, 1891), p. 181. And cf. B. Godfrey, "Sentencing, theatre, audience and communication: the Victorian and Edwardian magistrates' courts and their message", in B. Garnot (ed.), *Les témoins devant la justice* (Rennes, 2003), p. 168.

[252] *East London Advertizer*, 22 June 1898, p. 3; N. Tomes, "A 'Torrent of Abuse': Crimes of Violence Between Working-Class Men and Women in London, 1840-1875", *Journal of Social History*, vol. 11 (1978), p. 333.

feuds between neighbouring families. Women summonsed other women, arising from quarrels over children or domestic and sexual reputation. Costermongers were renowned for drink-induced fracas on Monday, after a long weekend of work. "In their anger they summon one another freely", said Booth, "but in the end will often subscribe to help their assailant to pay his fine." Even criminals were not averse to using the courts. The Coons, the biggest Jewish villains in the East End, went to Old Street court to ask for protection from Arthur Harding by way of information warrants. Harding was also fined £10 when his business partner, whom Harding had belted for being too fond of women, got a summons against him.[253]

Theft was initiated through a summons less frequently than assault charges, but working people were not averse to using the courts to deal with loss of property. Sons who stole from fathers, siblings robbed by siblings, landladies robbed by lodgers, all were taken before the East End courts. Parents were prepared to use the courts to put a shot across the bow of an errant child. Such youthful behaviour would ordinarily have been ignored or punished informally. Again, however, working-class prosecutors commonly declined to press theft charges through to conviction.[254]

In cases of child abuse, private charity entered the equation in the shape of the National Society for the Prevention of Cruelty to Children (NSPCC), "the Cruelty Men." The "Children's Charter" of 1889, along with amending acts in 1894 and 1904, criminalized intentional ill-treatment or neglect of children, and empowered policemen to take suspected child

---

[253] Ross, *Love and Toil*, p. 158; Booth, *Life and Labour*, Final Volume, p. 83; Samuel, *East End Underworld*, pp. 96, 152-4; J. Davis, "A Poor Man's System of Justice: The London Police Courts in the Second Half of the Nineteenth Century", *Historical Journal*, vol. 27 (1984), pp. 317-19, 321.

[254] Ross, "Fierce Questions and Taunts", pp. 584, 588; Ross, "Survival Networks", p. 15; Ross, *Love and Toil*, p. 161; Davis "Prosecutions and Their Context", note 57, p. 415, and p. 416. Note also that mothers commonly came to the police courts to plead for their children, illustrating that in the disciplining of young people, there was a popular willingness to negotiate with external agencies such as the police, schools, and courts.

victims from their homes. In March 1889, the metropolitan police commissioner had directed policemen to submit all cases of child cruelty to the NSPCC. When around 1893 the police found Charlie Chaplin and his brother asleep by a watchman's fire at three in the morning, they made the drunken stepmother take them in and passed the case to the NSPCC, which paid a visit to the home, much to the indignation of the stepmother.[255] The Society also dealt with cases of sexual abuse that the police passed to them, though only 11 per cent of the cruelty cases investigated by the East End branch in 1890 involved sexual abuse. While a quarter of the initial complaints to the Society about cruelty or neglect were made by police officers, teachers, School Board inspectors, and Poor Law officials, well over half were made by neighbours.[256] Neighbourhood self-sufficiency gave way increasingly to public willingness to use the child protection auxiliaries.

In June 1898, a Dalston shoemaker was charged at North London police court with violently assaulting his 12 year-old son. The father had been fined for the boy's truancy, so he had thrashed the boy with a leather strap. According to the report in the *Hackney Gazette*, "the neighbours interfered, and called in the police." In October 1897, the Limehouse coroner held an inquest on the body of an 11-year old boy, son of a warehouseman of Carr Street, whose death was alleged to have resulted from injuries inflicted by his father. An NSPCC inspector stated that he had prosecuted the father in 1894 for ill-treating three of his

---

[255] W. Moyle, "Inspecting London", in G. Sims (ed.), *Living London* (London, 1901), vol. 3, p. 239; G. Behlmer, *Child Abuse and Moral Reform in England, 1870-1908* (Stanford, 1982), pp. 162-3, 218-19; Ross, *Love and Toil*, p. 24; H. Hendrick, *Child Welfare. England 1872-1989* (London, 1994), p. 55; Behlmer, *Friends of the Family*, pp. 110-11; C. Chaplin, *My Autobiography* (New York, 1964), p. 40.

[256] Wise, *The Blackest Streets*, pp. 122, 127; Behlmer, *Friends of the Family*, pp. 104, 112; Davin, *Growing Up Poor*, note 50, p. 224; Behlmer, *Child Abuse*, pp. 170, 173; L.A. Jackson, *Child sexual abuse in Victorian England* (London, 2000), pp. 31, 61-64. Jackson argued that the law was mostly invoked in allegations of sexual abuse by strangers, lodgers, employers, or neighbours, much less so in the case of family members.

daughters. On that occasion, he had been convicted and bound over. To the consternation of the coroner, the jury returned a verdict of "death by misadventure", since the blow struck was not done with the intention of killing the boy. Even so, the father and mother were hooted outside the court. By this time, however, the percentage of NSPCC cases sent to a criminal court had fallen to below ten per cent, the Society preferring to use other restraints.[257]

By 1901, according to William Moyle, the uniformed 'cruelty man', many of whom were ex-policemen, was a familiar figure in London neighbourhoods, checking on progress at homes where a cautionary notice had been given, only occasionally delivering a summons for neglect or ill-treatment. Ernest Aves, in his report on Whitechapel, was impressed by the combined deterrent or punitive effect of the police and NSPCC. "It does many parents good", he wrote, "to see the officer of the Society for the Prevention of Cruelty to Children on his rounds, and to know what the initials on his cap mean." Booth affirmed that the influence of the NSPCC was "undoubtedly salutary as a check on neglect and cruelty", and that children were said to "threaten to appeal to it."[258]

Not only were the police courts a resource that the working poor were increasingly prepared to employ, but also a safeguard of sorts against the power wielded by the other agencies of social discipline, state or private. Magistrates by no means always sided with the police, the School Board, the Poor Law, or private charities. We have seen how East End magistrates locked horns with the police in cases of drunkenness, prostitution, and gambling. Montagu Williams was suspicious of police evidence; Albert Cluer gave prisoners the benefit of every doubt and openly criticized police decisions. In July 1893, Frederick Mead criticized the police for escorting a rent collector to evict a woman in Elsa Street, at the very time she was at

[257] *Hackney Gazette*, 15 June 1898, p. 3; *Daily News*, 2 Oct. 1897.
[258] Booth Collection, Religious Influences Series, A 39(8), ff. 11-12; Booth, *Life and Labour*, Final Volume, pp. 42-3.

Thames police court seeking the advice of the magistrate, and stated "the police by their presence lent colour to an illegal ejectment."[259]

Magistrates showed a similar independence of mind in relation to School Board, Poor Law, and Children's Society cases. Some constantly dismissed School Board prosecutions, or adjourned cases to see if attendance improved, or inflicted nominal fines. Williams was particularly renowned for thumbing his nose at the School Board, refusing to convict parents who had flagrantly and repetitively failed to send their children to school. In these ways, magistrates encouraged families to defy the School Board. In the execution of the law of compulsory school attendance, as Auerbach argued, "there still remained room for negotiation, contestation, and even outright evasion."[260] Mr. Dickinson chastised the Labour Master of Poplar Workhouse for

---

[259] For Cluer, see Samuel, *East End Underworld*, pp. 307-8; *East London Advertizer*, 12 March 1898, p. 5; *Hackney Gazette*, 16 March 1898, p. 4; *RC on Metropolitan Police*, Evidence, PP. 1908 [Cd. 4260], vol. L, pp. 67-75. Cluer provided examples of misconduct in the policing of street disorder for the Royal Commission to investigate. His relations with the police were so bad by this date that the Commission ignored his complaints. For Mead, see NA, MEPO 2/ 320

[260] Davin, *Growing Up Poor*, pp. 86-7; J. Lewis, "Parents, children, school fees and the London School Board 1870-1890", *History of Education*, vol. 11 (1982), p. 300; Philpott, *London At School*, p. 93; Rubinstein, "Socialization", p. 249 (for Montagu Williams); Rubinstein, *School Attendance*, pp. 98-102; Behlmer, *Friends of the Family*, pp. 99-100; S. Auerbach, "'The Law Has No Feeling for Poor Folks Like Us!': Everyday Responses to Legal Compulsion in England's Working-Class Communities, 1871-1904", *Journal of Social History*, vol. 45 (2012), p. 703. We should not overestimate, however, the sympathies of magistrates. During 1902-3, there were no fewer than 20,436 prosecutions of London parents for failing to send their children regularly to school, and few of these cases were dismissed. In addition, as Auerbach noted, the education laws "were among the first statutes that brought the reach of public authority and its agents into the working-class home on a daily basis", and as such expanded the role of the state in private life: "'Some Punishment Should Be Devised': Parents, Children, and the State in Victorian London", *Historian*, vol. 71 (2009), pp. 757-79. Some part of parental resistance to the introduction of compulsory school attendance surely drew from a desire to maintain authority in the home and to reject state authority: see Philpott, *London At School*, p. 195.

charging a man with neglecting to do his allotted task, to break 10 cwt of stones. Said Dickinson to the labour master, "you should discriminate in these cases. Here is a man who has only been used to playing a musical instrument … (To the prisoner): Go away; you are discharged." [261]

Parents concerned about the ill-treatment, visiting rights, or improper detention of their children in Dr. Barnardo's homes turned to the magistrates, who typically voiced support and occasionally encouraged the press to take up the cause. An officer of the Children's Aid Society charged a 13 year old girl with being found wandering in Dod Street, Limehouse, and not under proper guardianship, asking the court to send her to a reformatory. Mr. Mead's cross-examination of the rescue officer revealed that he had gone to the house where the girl was living and arranged that she be put into the street in order to justify the charge of wandering. Mead discharged the girl, telling her she would be trained and found a good situation. Indeed, magistrates were never eager to send children to penal institutions. Inspector Barker of Bethnal Green told Duckworth that there was no Industrial School for Jewish boys, and since magistrates were reluctant to send boys under 14 to Reformatory Schools, they discharged them instead. [262]

In sum, the police courts were used by ordinary people to shape, define, and enforce the moral codes of their own communities, and as sites for resistance to official visions of community order. [263] East Enders "went to law" against each other to handle petty thefts, domestic violence, or mistreatment of children, against employers who refused to pay them or give them

---

[261] *The Illustrated Police News*, 1 May 1897.

[262] L. Murdoch, *Imagined Orphans. Poor Families, Child Welfare, and Contested Citizenship in London* (New Brunswick, 2006), pp. 110-14; *The Pall Mall Gazette*, 2 July 1898; *Reynolds's Newspaper*, 3 July 1898; Police Walks, B 352, f. 61 (Barker). In addition to the cases of social discipline examined above, the police courts were deeply involved in the revolt against vaccination in the East End: *East London Advertiser*, 1 Jan. 1898.

[263] Cf. B. Yngvesson, "Inventing Law in Local Settings: Rethinking Popular Legal Culture", *Yale Law Journal*, vol. 98 (1989), pp. 1690, 1693-95, 1698, 1709.

adequate notice of dismissal, and against landlords who sought to evict them or charge them exorbitant rents. As Michael Ignatieff observed, the courts should be understood "as only the official and visible end-point of a process of popular justice which began within the working class communities."[264] It is possible, too, that the police courts played a part in re-defining the content and boundaries of popular conduct. Martin Wiener has argued that the higher courts' greater severity against men who maimed and killed women helped to reconfigure masculinity, to diminish male aggression, and to propagate a new sensibility of inhibition and self-discipline. This "civilizing offensive" may have filtered down to police court level where magistrates dealt with the bulk of assault cases. Canon Barnett thought the police courts in each district were "'the very center of observation and information', " and press accounts of cases aroused an interest exceeded only by sporting news.[265] The press was selective in the cases it reported, however, so it is unclear what messages were heard. It is even harder to know if the messages were internalized; if the courts served to inform and influence popular behaviour.[266] We should conclude only that the poor took a pragmatic, instrumental view of what the police courts could offer, and used them in conjunction with the popular framework of rituals, rules, values, and cultural inhibitions. East Enders were not the passive objects of law; they were active subjects in negotiations between the police, the courts, state and voluntary agencies, and each other — and as such, vital to the construction of the social order.[267]

---

[264] M. Ignatieff, "Total Institutions and Working Classes: A Review Essay", *History Workshop*, Issue 15 (1983), p. 170.

[265] M. Wiener, *Men of Blood: Violence, Manliness and Criminal Justice in Victorian England* (Cambridge, 2004); B.S. Godfrey, et al, "Explaining Gendered Sentencing Patterns for Violent Men and Women in the Late-Victorian and Edwardian Period", *British Journal of Criminology*, vol. 45 (2005), pp. 717-18; Tomes, "A Torrent of Abuse", pp. 338-41; Barnett cited in Behlmer, *Friends of the Family*, p. 189. Tomes showed that London magistrates were increasingly intolerant of assaults on females and willing to give harsher sentences.

[266] Cf. Godfrey, "Sentencing, theatre, audience", p. 170.

[267] The argument here is not that popular use of the courts represented consent to the law as distinct from coercion by the law. The police courts were a

XIV

I remain unconvinced by a description of Victorian England as a "policeman-state." Not even in the East End of London, surely the toughest test case imaginable, is the description valid. The metropolitan police were trained to do too little rather than too much, were pretty much excluded from home and workplace, were cautious about offending the people they policed, and were unwilling to bow to external pressure to expand surveillance over offences they found next to impossible to prevent. Police were not the prime movers in the control of deviant behaviour. They worked at the margins; they acted as a continuation of efforts by the mass of the population to maintain order. Policing was a backstop to the social and cultural processes through which conformity was induced. Proper conduct on a regular and consistent basis owed anywhere near as much to other structural and cultural arrangements, to spheres of authority that were contextual, contingent, and local. Order was cemented less by policing than by a complex combination of informal family and community sanctions, the mixed welfare of charity and state support, the new board schools, slum clearance, and the negotiated justice of the police courts.

This should lead us to question the role of the state in the making of social order, or at least the assumption that the state is all-powerful. We have been persuaded that the pacification of modern society was an institutional achievement, the work of policemen, magistrates, and prison guards, a triumph of specialist law enforcement. We have been persuaded that the private actions of ordinary people were unimportant; the spontaneous processes of popular enforcement irrelevant. In fact, the imposition of police power in the nineteenth century did not inevitably take place at the expense of informal social control. State sanctioning did not inevitably weaken subordinate sanctioning. It all suggests that today's police forces will do well

---

coercive instrument of the state, and people used them to employ power in the resolution of their disputes. It is to argue that popular use of the courts suggests that coercion and consent were complexly interwoven.

to recognize that they can be effective only by working with, through, and on the other mechanisms of control in society.

Aliens Act of 1905, 102-103
anti-alien movement, 100-101,
    102-103, 104
assaults, 1, 38n87, 87, 126, 127,
    128-129, 130, 135, 135n265
Auerbach, S., 133, 133n260
August, Andrew, 63n137, 71

Barnett, Henrietta, 84, 86-87
Barnett, Samuel, 37n84, 86, 92n188,
    121-122, 135
begging, 22, 23-24, 24n51, 128
Besant, Walter, 9
Bethnal Green
    in Booth classification of London
      streets, 15-16
    charity in, 113-116
    children in, 118
    crime in, 27, 29-30, 34n80, 43
    drinking and drunkenness in, 47,
      48n111, 50n114, 51
    East End location of, 6-7, 7
      (illustration)
    Jewish population in, 98, 101
    occupations in, 71n151
    police courts in, 126
    policing of, 20, 27
    popular codes of alternate policing
      in, 77-78, 79, 80, 84
    prostitution in, 59
    and publicans' bribing of police, 53,
      53-54n120, 55
    slum clearance in, 123, 125
    truancy in, 119
    working class in, 7-8, 8n17
betting shops, 61, 65n141. *See also*
    gambling
Board Schools, 17n37, 117, 117n228,
    118-121, 120n235, 122. *See also*
    education and schools
Booth, Charles
    Life and Labour of the People in
      London by, 10-11, 10n22, 11n23,
      13, 15, 25
    and Poverty series, 9-11, 10n22, 89,
      94, 120n235

    and Religious Influences series,
      10-11, 11n23
    social classification of London
      streets by, 12-13, 13n27, 14-16,
      16n34, 86, 89, 112-114,
      123-124
    See also East End, London; police
      walks
Boundary Street Estate, 30-31,
    30n67, 101, 123, 124-125. *See*
    also slum clearance
Bourdieu, Pierre, 5
Bourke, Joanna, 74-75
Bow, 6-7, 8, 64, 71n151, 80-81
Bradford, Edward, 11, 14, 14n29,
    35-36, 36n82
Brodie, Marc, 89-90
Bromley, 6-7, 8, 48, 54-55, 71n151
brothels, 58-59, 60-61, 61n132, 67,
    72, 88, 102. *See also* prostitution

charities and social services, 110-115,
    115n222
Charity Organization Society,
    115n222
child abuse, 79, 125, 130-132,
    131n256
child labour, 118, 122
child prostitution, 56
Chrisp Street Market, 92, 93 (photo)
churches. *See* charities and social
    services; religion
Coles, Frances, 104, 104n206, 106
    (illustration), 117
community solidarity, working-class
    conditions supporting, 75-76,
    76n158, 76n159
    consensus and power relations
      within, 74-75
    and informal codes of behaviour
      and alternate policing, 5-6, 76-82,
      81n171, 84-87, 85-86n176,
      90-92, 90n184, 91n186
    and informal responsibility for
      social welfare, 76-77
    "rough" v. "respectable" in, 88-93,

INDEX

91n186
and social welfare role of police,
82-83
costermongers (street traders), 8, 24,
32-33, 38, 70, 85, 130
courts. *See* police courts
crime
assaults, 1, 38n87, 87, 126, 127,
128-129, 130, 135, 135n265
and decline in crime reports to
police, 80
and decline of recorded crime in
Victorian England, 1-6, 1n1, 2n3,
2n4, 3n9, 4n11, 4-5n12
education and, 39n91
and habitual criminals, 41-45,
44n105, 45n106
and Jack-the-Ripper, 9, 37n84, 96,
104, 104n206, 106 (illustration),
109, 117
Jewish East End population and,
103-108, 103n204
among juveniles, 26n53, 103, 118
and lodging-houses, 31-32, 34,
34n79, 34n80, 40, 42, 59, 87,
125n244
murder, 32, 56, 80, 87, 104
political economy of, 84
robberies and burglaries, 1, 41, 87,
103, 125
ticket-of-leave men and, 28, 30, 34,
41, 42-44, 44n104, 105
and working-class solidarity, 92
See also drunkenness, drinking and;
gambling; prostitution

Davis, Jennifer, 2n4, 126
Dennis, Richard, 16n34
Dickens, Charles, 34n79, 122
District Boards of Works, 121-122
Dock Strike (1889), 17, 73, 74
(photo), 74n155
dockworkers, 29, 33, 46, 70, 71-72,
71n151, 73, 97, 100n199, 116
domestic violence, 15, 79-80, 87,
126, 128, 134-135

"Donkey Row," 28, 34, 48, 75-76,
108
Doyle, Arthur Conan, 117n228, 125
Dr. Barnardo's homes for destitute
children, 83, 115, 134
drunkenness, drinking and
decline in prosecutions for, 1
in East End neighbourhoods, 47-51,
47n109, 48n111, 50n114
and Licensing Act of 1902, 49
among police, 53, 53n119, 55
police courts and, 50n114, 51-52,
52n117
policing of, 48-53, 50n114, 54-55
and publicans' bribery of police,
52-55, 53-54n120
among women, 47-48, 49
Duckworth, George, police walks
and, 12-15, 13n27, 14n30, 25

East End, London
and Booth Poverty series, 9-11,
10n22, 89, 94, 120n235
ethnic homogeneity in, 8
geographic borders of, 6-7, 7
(illustration), 7n16
as laboratory for social reformers
and philanthropists, 8-10, 9n18,
10n22
working class in, 7-8, 8n17, 29
See also individual neighbourhoods
by name
East London Defence Alliance, 9n18
education and schools
and Board Schools, 17n37, 117,
117n228, 118-121, 120n235, 122
and compulsory school attendance,
118-120, 120n235, 125, 126,
133, 133n260
and crime, 39n91
and impact on working classes, 112,
117-122, 117n228
and industrial schools, 103, 111,
118, 120, 134
Education Act of 1870, 118-119
employment. *See* occupations and

INDEX

trades
Endacott-Cass case, 56, 57, 59-60
Englander, David, 100n199, 115-117
ethnic communities, 94. *See also* Irish
  population; Jewish population
ex-convicts. *See* habitual criminals;
  ticket-of-leave men

factories, women workers in, 29, 70,
  80-81, 81n171, 81 (photo)
family, 69, 76-77, 79-80, 90, 90n184,
  108-109,111, 136. *See also*
  community solidarity,
  working-class
Fenian Barracks, 15, 17n35, 32, 64,
  119
friendly societies, 46, 90, 90-91n184

gambling
  and betting shops, 61, 65n141
  among Jewish population, 62, 66,
    101-102
  legislation against, 61-62, 64
  police and, 45-46, 61-62, 63,
    63n137, 64-65, 66-68, 84, 85, 87
  police courts and, 45, 61, 64, 65,
    65n141, 65n142, 126, 127, 128,
    132
  in public houses, 64
  and street betting, 61-62, 63-64
  among women, 65, 65n141
Gatrell, Vic, 3-4, 4n11, 25n52, 39,
  40-41

habitual criminals, 41-45, 44n105,
  45n106. *See also* ticket-of-leave
  men
Habitual Criminals Act of 1869,
  41-42, 44-45
Hackney, 6-7, 7 (illustration), 11, 14,
  47n109, 62, 64, 113
Haggerston, 26n53, 27
Harding, Arthur, 26n55, 30n66, 112
  in the courts, 130
  as an habitual criminal, 42, 43, 88
  on Jewish crime, 102, 103,
    107n211

on police corruption, 39, 39n90,
    40-41, 66
  and police relationship with the
    poor, 83
  and political economy of crime, 84
  on tenement houses, 31n69
Harris, Jose, 69
Hobbs, Dick, 6n15, 39
Hobsbawm, E. J., 76-77
homelessness, 24, 24n51, 38-39, 120
housing, 6, 9, 11n24, 69-70, 100,
    101, 111, 123-124. *See also*
    lodging-houses; slum clearance
Hoxton, 25-27, 26n53, 30, 40, 55,
    71n151, 83, 91

Ignatieff, Michael, 5, 135
illegitimacy, 78
immigrants, 6, 8, 11n24, 73, 94,
    100n199, 102, 105. *See also* Irish
    population; Jewish population
Irish population, 27, 32-34, 59, 91,
    94, 97, 100, 105, 107, 119
Isle of Dogs, 11, 29, 47, 63-64,
    71n151, 112

Jack-the-Ripper, 9, 37n84, 96, 104,
    104n206, 106 (illustration), 109,
    117
Jackson, Louise, 125n244, 131n256
Jewish Association for the Protection
    of Girls and Women, 103n204,
    111
Jewish Board of Guardians, 110-111
Jewish Ladies' Association for
    Preventive and Rescue Work, 102
Jewish population
  anarchists among, 105
  anti-alien movement and, 100-101,
    102-103
  and crime, 103-109, 103n204
  and gambling, 62, 66, 101-102
  geographical and cultural
    characteristics of, 95-98, 97
    (illustration), 98-99n197,
    100-101,

141

INDEX

100n199, 107-109, 110 (photo)
George Duckworth on, 95-97, 107
immigration of, 95-96
labour and trades among, 8, 98,
98-99n197, 99 (photo)
police courts and, 104, 130
policing of, 99-100, 101-102,
103-107, 107n211, 111
and prostitution, 102-103, 103n204
and social order, 95, 96n193, 97,
99-101, 102, 107-109
social services available to, 110-111
women in, 95-96, 103n204, 109
juvenile crime, 26n53, 103, 118

labour, organized, 63n137, 72-73, 73
(photo), 99n198, 105
labour productivity, 71n151, 72
LCC. *See* London County Council
(LCC)
Lees, Lynn Hollen, 116-117
Lewis, H. S., 95, 95n192, 96,
98-99n197, 100n199, 103
Licensing Act of 1902, 49
*Life and Labour of the People in
London. See* Booth, Charles
Limehouse
drunkenness in, 47
East End location of, 6-7, 71n151
ethnic communities in, 94
gambling in, 28, 65n141
and improvements in labour
conditions, 72
and local government, 122
and police and public relationship,
68
police court serving, 126
prostitution in, 59, 60
"rough" area of, 27, 28, 34, 48,
75-76, 108
wage relationship and social order
in, 70
working-class population in,
71n151
living standards, improved, 69-70
local government, 23, 56, 61-62, 112,

177, 121-122, 136-137. *See also*
education and schools;
slum clearance
lodging-houses
clearance of, 31-32, 123n240
criminals and, 31-32, 34, 34n79,
34n80, 40, 42, 59, 87, 125n244
and police informants, 15, 40
police inspection of, 24, 24n51
prostitution and, 59, 125n244
supervision of, 122
in Whitechapel, 24n51, 31-32,
34n80, 39, 125n244
women in, 24n51
London County Council (LCC), 30,
30n67, 62, 91n186, 113n218,
122, 123
London East End. *See* East End,
London
London Poverty Maps (1889), 12-13,
12 (illustration), 16, 86
London Public Morality Council, 57
London Times, 3, 86
Lotteries and Betting Act of 1853, 61

magistrates. *See* police courts
Mayhew, Henry, 7n16
Mayne, Richard, 23
McKibbin, Ross, 63n137
Metropolitan Police Act of 1839, 23,
56
Metropolitan Streets Act of 1867,
61-62
middle-class population, 8n17,
74n155
Middlesex Street, 99 (photo)
Mile End Old Town, 6-7, 7
(illustration), 71n151, 102, 111,
114, 115n222
"model" block dwellings, 18, 31-32,
107, 114-115, 122-125,
123n241, 125n244. *See also*
lodging-houses; slum clearance
morals offenses, 4, 4-5n12, 13. *See
also* drunkenness, drinking and;
gambling; prostitution

142

Ralph Anstis, Warren James and the Dean Forest Riots, *The Disturbances of 1831*
£14.00 • 242pp *paperback* • 191x235mm • ISBN 978-0-9564827-7-8

The full story of the riots in the Forest of Dean in 1831, and how they were suppressed, is told here for the first time. Dominating the story is the enigmatic character of Warren James, the self-educated free miner who led the foresters in their attempt to stave off their increasing poverty and unemployment, and to protect their traditional way life from the threats of advancing industrial change.

John E. Archer, 'By a Flash and a Scare', *Arson, Animal Maiming, and Poaching in East Anglia 1815-1870*
£12.00 • 206pp *paperback* • 191x235mm • ISBN 978-0-9564827-1-6

'By a Flash and a Scare' illuminates the darker side of rural life in the nineteenth century. Flashpoints such as the Swing riots, Tolpuddle, and the New Poor Law riots have long attracted the attention of historians, but here John E. Archer focuses on the persistent war waged in the countryside during the 1800s, analysing the prevailing climate of unrest, discontent, and desperation.

Victor Bailey, Order and Disorder in Modern Britain, *Essays on Riot, Crime, Policing and Punishment*
£15.00 • 214pp *paperback* • 5 *b/w images* • 191x235mm • ISBN 978-0-9570005-5-1

The pieces in this collection range from an account of the Skeleton Army riots against the Salvation Army in the early 1880s to the unsuccessful campaign to abolish the death penalty in the aftermath of the Second World War. They include essays on how the Home Office and Metropolitan Police responded to the unemployed riots in the West End of London in 1886 and the contest over the right to assemble in Trafalgar Square in 1887; on the complex relationship between the Salvation Army's social scheme and the early labour movement; on the changing meanings inscribed within the term "dangerous and criminal classes"; and on English penal culture from the Gladstone Committee's Report on Prisons (1895) to the Labour Research Department's Prison System Enquiry Committee's report, English Prisons Today (1922).

The essays in this volume, (first published between 1977 and 2000), are coherent expressions, if not of a single philosophy, at least of a recurrent theme. That theme is the relationship between order and disorder in England over the century from 1850. Despite the stress fractures caused by deepening industrialization, strengthening class mobilization, and cyclical economic dislocation, Britain was a relatively peaceable kingdom in these years. Who and what were responsible for the imposition of social order?

In these essays, the emphasis is less on coercive policing, less on the conditioning of the working poor by 'moral entrepreneurs' into a set of desirable behaviours — though these doubtless played their part — and much more on the role of informal and autonomous communal and class codes; on the social and moral differentiation between the 'respectable working class' and the 'residuum', a normative ditch working people helped to dig and guard; and on popular support for, or at least popular participation in, the formal mechanisms of law and punishment.

Bob Bushaway, By Rite, *Custom, Ceremony and Community in England 1700-1880*
£14.00 • 206pp *paperback* • 191x235mm • ISBN 978-0-9564827-6-1

Political philosophers (such as Gramsci) and social historians (such as E. P. Thompson) have suggested that rural customs and ceremonies have much more to them than the picturesqueness which has attracted traditional folklorists. They can be seen to have a purpose in the structures of rural society. But no historian has really pursued this idea for the English folk materials of the eighteenth and nineteenth centuries: the period from which most evidence survives.

Bringing together a wealth of research, this book explores the view that rural folk practices were a mechanism of social cohesion, and social disruption. Through them the interdependence of the rural working-class and the gentry was affirmed, and infringements of the rights of the poor resisted, sometimes aggressively.

Malcolm Chase, The People's Farm, *English Radical Agrarianism 1775-1840*
£12.00 • 212pp *paperback* • 152x229mm • ISBN 978-0-9564827-5-4

This book traces the development of agrarian ideas from the 1770s through to Chartism, and seeks to explain why, in an era of industrialization and urban growth, land remained one of the major issues in popular politics. Malcolm Chase considers the relationship between 'land consciousness' and early socialism; attempts to create alternative communities; and contemporary perceptions of nature and the environment. *The People's Farm* also provides the most extensive study to date of Thomas Spence, and his followers the Spenceans.

Malcolm Chase, Early Trade Unionism, *Fraternity, Skill and the Politics of Labour*
£14.00 • 248pp *paperback* • 191x235mm • ISBN 978-0-9570005-2-0

Once the heartland of British labour history, trade unionism has been marginalised in much recent scholarship. In a critical survey from the earliest times to the nineteenth century, this book argues for its reinstatement. Trade unionism is shown to be both intrinsically important and to provide a window onto the broader historical landscape; the evolution of trade union principles and practices is traced from the seventeenth century to mid-Victorian times. Underpinning this survey is an explanation of labour organisation that reaches back to the fourteenth century. Throughout, the emphasis is on trade union mentality and ideology, rather than on institutional history. There is a critical focus on the politics of gender, on the demarcation of skill and on the role of the state in labour issues. New insight is provided on the long-debated question of trade unions' contribution to social and political unrest from the era of the French Revolution through to Chartism.

BREVIARY STUFF PUBLICATIONS
www.breviarystuff.org.uk

Nigel Costley, West Country Rebels
£20.00 • 220pp *full colour illustrated paperback* • 216x216mm • ISBN
978-0-9570005-4-4

What comes to mind when you think of the West Country? Beautiful beaches and
coastline perhaps, rich countryside and moorland, great historic sites such as Stonehenge
or perhaps the grace of Regency Bath or the stunning design of Brunel's Clifton
Suspension Bridge? You may think of the West Country as the peaceful, quiet corner of
Britain where people visit for holidays or spend their retirement.

What may not spring to mind is the Western Rebellion against enclosures, the
bloody battles for fair taxes, the Prayer Book Rebellion against an imposed English Bible,
the turbulent years of the Civil War and the Monmouth Rebellion that ended with the
ruthless revenge of Judge Jefferies. You may know little about the radical edge to the
region's maritime past such as the naval mutinies, smuggling and struggle for safety.

The West Country was famous for its wool and cloth but the battles by textile
workers is less well known. For generations communities around the South West organised
and engaged in riot and uprising, for food, for access, for fair tax and to be heard in a
society that denied most people the vote. Women were at the centre of many of these
disputes and their battle with poverty and inequality is featured along with West Country
women who challenged those that kept them out and held them back.   Trade   unionism
has many a West Country story to tell, from the Tolpuddle Martyrs in Dorset, the longest
strike in Plymouth, the great china clay strike of 1913, 'Black Friday' in Bristol and the
battle for rights at GCHQ in Cheltenham..

This book features these struggles along with the characters who defied convention
and helped organise around dangerous ideas of freedom, equality and justice.

Barry Reay, The Last Rising of the Agricultural Labourers, *Rural Life and
Protest in Nineteenth-Century England*

£12.00 • 192pp *paperback* • 191x235mm • ISBN 978-0-9564827-2-3

The Hernhill Rising of 1838 was the last battle fought on English soil, the last revolt
against the New Poor Law, and England's last millenarian rising. The bloody 'Battle of
Bosenden Wood', fought in a corner of rural Kent, was the culmination of a revolt led by
the self-styled 'Sir William Courtenay'. It was also, despite the greater fame of the 1830
Swing Riots, the last rising of the agricultural labourers.

Buchanan Sharp, In Contempt of All Authority, *Rural Artisans and Riot in the
West of England, 1586-1660*
£12.00 • 204pp *paperback* • 191x235mm • ISBN 978-0-9564827-0-9

Two of the most common types of popular disorders in late Tudor and early Stuart
England were the food riots and the anti-enclosure riots in royal forests. Of particular
interest are the forest riots known collectively as the Western Rising of 1626-1632, and
the lesser known disorders in the Western forests which took place during the English
Civil War. The central aims of this volume are to establish the social status of the people
who engaged in those riots and to determine the social and economic conditions which
produced the disorders.

BREVIARY STUFF PUBLICATIONS
www.breviarystuff.org.uk

Dorothy Thompson, The Chartists, *Popular Politics in the Industrial Revolution*
£16.00 • 280pp *paperback* • 191x235mm • ISBN 978-0-9570005-3-7

The Chartists is a major contribution to our understanding not just of Chartism but of the whole experience of working-class people in mid-nineteenth century Britain. The book looks at who the Chartists were, what they hoped for from the political power they strove to gain, and why so many of them felt driven toward the use of physical force. It also studies the reactions of the middle and upper classes and the ways in which the two sides — radical and establishment — influenced each other's positions.

The book is a uniquely authoritative discussion of the questions that Chartism raises for the historian; and for the historian, student and general reader alike it provides a vivid insight into the lives of working people as they passed through the traumas of the industrial revolution.

E. P. Thompson, Whigs and Hunters, *The Origin of the Black Act*
£16.00 • 278pp *paperback* • 156x234mm • ISBN 978-0-9570005-2-0

With *Whigs and Hunters*, the author of *The Making of the English Working Class*, E. P. Thompson plunged into the murky waters of the early eighteenth century to chart the violently conflicting currents that boiled beneath the apparent calm of the time. The subject is the Black Act, a law of unprecedented savagery passed by Parliament in 1723 to deal with 'wicked and evil-disposed men going armed in disguise'. These men were pillaging the royal forest of deer, conducting a running battle against the forest officers with blackmail, threats and violence.

These 'Blacks', however, were men of some substance; their protest (for such it was) took issue with the equally wholsesale plunder of the forest by Whig nominees to the forest offices. And Robert Walpole, still consolidating his power, took an active part in the prosecution of the 'Blacks'. The episode is laden with political and social implications, affording us glimpses of considerable popular discontent, political chicanery, judicial inequity, corrupt ambition and crime.

David Walsh, Making Angels in Marble, *The Conservatives, the Early Industrial Working Class and Attempts at Political Incorporation*
£15.00 • 268pp *paperback* • 191x235mm • ISBN 978-0-9570005-0-6

In the first elections called under the terms of the 1832 Reform Act the Tory party appeared doomed. They had recorded their worst set of results in living memory and were organizationally in disarray as well, importantly, seemingly completely out of touch with the current political mood. During the intense pressure brought to bear by the supporters of political reform was the use of "pressure from without" and in this tactic the industrial working class were highly visible. Calls for political reform had been growing since the 1760s and given fresh impetus with the revolutions in America and France respectively. The old Tory party had been resistant to all but the most glaring corruption and abuse under the pre-Reform system, not least to the idea of extending the electoral franchise to the 'swineish multitude', as Edmund Burke notoriously described the working class. Yet within five years after the passing of reform the Conservatives — the natural heirs to the old Tory party — were attempting to politically incorporate sections of the working class into their ranks. This book examines how this process of making these 'Angels in Marble', to use Disraeli's phrase from a later era, took shape in the 1830s. It focuses on how a section of the industrial working class became the target of organizational inclusion into Peelite Conservatism and ultimately into the British party political system.

BREVIARY STUFF PUBLICATIONS
www.breviarystuff.org.uk

Roger Wells, Insurrection, *The British Experience 1795-1803*
£17.50 • 372pp *paperback* • 191x235mm • ISBN 978-0-9564827-3-0

On the 16 November 1802 a posse of Bow Street Runners raided the Oakley Arms, a working class pub in Lambeth, on the orders of the Home Office. Over thirty men were arrested, among them, and the only one of any social rank, Colonel Edward Marcus Despard. Despard and twelve of his associates were subsequently tried for high treason before a Special Commission, and Despard and six others were executed on 21 February 1803. It was alleged that they had planned to kill the King, seize London and overturn the government and constitution.

Until recently this event had been almost entirely neglected by historians, principally on the grounds that it was an *isolated* occurrence, the brainchild of a disgruntled and probably insane Irishman. The incident is relegated to a footnote in the relevant volume of the *Oxford History of England* and even then only in support of First Minister Addington's habitual 'calmness'.

The first coherent reappraisal of the Despard affair was provided by E. P. Thompson, in his magnificent work, *The Making of the English Working Class*. An integral part of Thompson's thesis hinges on his analysis of what happened to one seminal political development in the 1790s, namely the first primarily English working-class movement for democracy. E. P. Thompson's claim that determined physical force revolutionary groupings originated after the suppression of the Popular Democratic Movement in 1795 has been seriously challenged by conventional British historians. This book offers a reinterpretation of Thompson's evidence, through a detailed overall study of post-1795 British politics. It throws new light on the organisation of government intelligence sources, Pitt's repressive policies and machinery, and oscillating popular responses; all developments, including recrudescences of the open Democratic Movement, and notably the emergence of insurrectionary conspiracies, are firmly related to both events in the critical Irish theatre, and the course of the war against France.

Roger Wells, Wretched Faces, *Famine in Wartime England 1793-1801*
£18.00 • 412pp *paperback* • 191x235mm • ISBN 978-0-9564827-4-7

This book reverts Malthus in a thoroughly English context. It proves that famine could, and did, occur in England during the classic period of the Industrial Revolution. The key economic determinant proved to be the ideologically-inspired war, orchestrated by the Prime Minister, the younger Pitt, against the French and their attempted export of revolutionary principles at bayonet point, to the rest of Europe. This international context, in part, conditioned the recurrent development of famine conditions in England in 1794-6 and again in 1799-1801. Here the multiple ramifications of famine in this country, as it lurched from crisis to crisis in wartime, are explored in considerable depth. These were repeated crises of capitalism, juxtaposed with the autocratic and aristocratic state's total ' commitment to war, which contrived to challenge not just the commitment to war, but both the equilibrium and the survival of the state itself. 'WANT' stalked the land; intense rioting periodically erupted; radical politicisation, notably of unenfranchised working people, proceeded apace, in part stimulated by the catastrophic events projected on the world stage by the process of the French Revolution. The book finally explains how such an oligarchic, unrepresentative government managed through determined economic interventionism, manipulation of the unique English social security system, and final resort to army rule, to preserve itself and the political structure during a key epoch within the Age of Revolutions.

www.ingramcontent.com/pod-product-compliance
Lightning Source LLC
Chambersburg PA
CBHW050526270326
41926CB00015B/3095